FINDING MY PURPOSE THROUGH PAIN

An Inspirational Story
By:

_____

Leda S. Porter

Tawanna!
Please enjoy my
the story ....flaws + all!
life.... God bless!

Leda

Finding My Purpose Through Pain
Copyright © 2016 by Leda S. Porter

ISBN: 1542680832

Dedication

I would like to dedicate this book to my children: Emily, Emmanuel, and Lydia. If it were not for you, I would not have the motivation to keep striving for greatness. When I felt that I was at my lowest point in life, I found hope in you. From the moment each of you all were born, my purpose changed. It was no longer about me. I had three little people depending on me for everything. I had to delay goals and aspirations; but I never gave up. Regardless of what life has thrown at me, you were the reason for my determination. With God's help, we've made it; and something that has been a dream for so long is now a reality. I truly believe through all the pain, there is no greater purpose than being your mother. I hope that I've made you all proud.

Table of Contents

Introduction

I had been struggling with finding my purpose in life for many years, only to realize God told me my purpose years ago. I was young and didn't quite understand what I was supposed to do then. So, here I am now fulfilling my promise to God and embarking upon His purpose in my life. I will share these words of this book written out of hurt, fear, loss, suffering, depression, and ultimately my rebirth.

When I think about my life, I often reflect on the times when I was hurt the most. I know that seems a bit unusual, but those times remind me of how far I've come. As a little girl, I was always kind of different; and as I matured, I spent a lot of time day dreaming, reading, and letting my imagination run wild. I remember being in school once and a teacher saying, "Your imagination can take you anywhere you want to go!" That stuck with me, even to this very day. It was around that time that I started writing. I just fell in love with the idea of using my imagination to write. By the time I neared the end of high school, one of my goals was to become a published author. Well, here I am today finally fulfilling that dream.

This book has been a part of me for as long as I could remember. Throughout my life, I've had many experiences, some of which defined who I am today. Those experiences ultimately led me to write this book to share my heart and how God restored me after hitting what I describe as rock bottom. I share pieces of my life--the highs and lows--and I relate ultimately how my faith helped me reach a level in Christ I never imagined possible. This book focuses on trusting God in your darkest hour when you feel your life and/or situation is beyond repair.

I have learned, as a single mother, that life can sometimes seem to get the best of you. I have spent many days crying and feeling helpless because I thought my situation was hopeless. Over the years, I've always found myself doing things just to provide for my family. As time progressed, I started to feel like I just "settled in" to life. I felt like I wasn't walking in my purpose. I knew God had more for me to do than being a mental health therapist or a mental health consultant. I am so blessed to have the career that God has given me, but it isn't fulfilling my purpose. When I realized I wanted to share my story and I started writing about it, it just felt right. I am so excited to share these words that are written from my heart. I hope to inspire other women, especially single parents to never give up on your dreams. If you hold on to your faith and trust God through whatever circumstances you encounter, you can overcome any obstacle!

Chapter One: The Early Years

I guess you can say I had pain throughout my childhood. I grew up in a home with my mom, dad, and three siblings. To the outside world, we seemed like the normal family; but that wasn't so. My dad was abusive to my mom; he abused her both verbally and physically. I suppose amid that, she had some significant mental abuse as well. I remember as a kid how angry my dad would get over little things. My mom would never defend herself; she just took it. I tried to figure out what was wrong with my dad. I wanted to understand why would he want to hurt my mom? She was a stay-at-home mother; she kept the house clean and she cooked every day. I don't think that mattered, though, because my dad always seemed to abuse her.

I recall the last time he abused her. I had to be about seven or eight- years-old. My mom had started going to church more after she got saved, and my dad didn't like it. He accused her of having an affair with a local preacher whose church my mom was attending. My dad was brutal. He abused my mom in front of us and in front of his mom, and he seemingly didn't care. Well, the last instance occurred when my dad had to go away to summer camp and my mom wasn't home. I think she was at church, so my dad had to pick up my grandmother to stay with us. He was furious because he was going to be late. Just as he was preparing his luggage to leave, my mom walked in the house. I remember that he started yelling, asking her where she'd been, and proceeding to abuse her. My mom just took it. I

1

don't think she could respond. After that incident, my mom left my dad and that's when things changed. It seemed like we were no longer a family.

My mom moved to her mother's house across town. At that point, my parents were officially separated. Mom stayed with grandmother and we eventually moved there, too. My dad picked us up for school every day and allowed us to stopped by the store on the way to school. I don't recall my dad talking much, but he let us have whatever we wanted at the store, which was usually some kind of pastry, a drink, and a snack for school. I don't remember how long we stayed with my grandmother but sometime later, we moved away from that small town to Columbus, about 30 miles north. I think my mom was ecstatic about getting a fresh start and getting away from my dad, or so she thought. I recall her telling us not to tell him where we lived or give him our phone number. I was so young, but I remember thinking, "How am I ever going to see my daddy? How am I going to talk to him?" I was saddened by the whole thing.

We moved into our new rental house on the North side of town and my mom had to register us for our new schools. I was so nervous because I wasn't sure what to expect. We had moved away from all our family, including my aunt, who was my teacher, and from all my friends. I didn't want to start over, but I was just a kid; no one would listen to me. I had to walk to my new school because we lived just around the corner. I walked with my sisters and my neighbor who was in my grade. We quickly became friends. I was starting to like our new home.

One day not long after we moved, I was walking home and I saw a car parked in front of our house. I realized it was my dad's car. I took off running! I was so happy to see him because I was a daddy's girl. I didn't know how he found us and I didn't say anything, but I was so glad to see him. He took us out to eat. We usually would go to McDonald's or Captain D's; those were our favorite places. My dad was a man of few words when he was around us. He usually talked about school, reminding us it was important to get good grades and go to college. I didn't care; I was just happy to see my dad.

We stayed in that house on the North side for a year or so. Then one day my mom said we were moving into another rental house on the East side of town. We stayed there for some time, but then we moved back to the North side of town. At some point between my third and sixth grade years, my parents were officially divorced. However, no matter where we moved, my dad always found us. When we moved back to the North side of town, on a dead-end street, near the projects, it seemed as if my dad knew everyone in that little neighborhood. My mom didn't want to change my school, so I didn't have to walk to the school in my new neighborhood; she drove me to my school in the old neighborhood, instead. The place we were living in was kind of scary, but my mom believed God that we would have our own house one day soon. I didn't like the new house on the North side, but I did get used to it. My mom went to a rummage sale once and she came back with a school desk. I used to sit in that desk and let my imagination run wild. I pretended to be a teacher or Whitney Houston. I would sit there and write or draw. I think that was my fondest memory of that house.

When my parents were married, there was always so much confusion because my dad was mean. He was a good parent, but he wasn't a good husband. I can recall that he was dating my fourth-grade teacher at some point. Imagine that? We stayed in the dead-end house on North side for more than a year and then we moved again. This time we moved all the way out to what I called 'the boon docks.' So much for the city life!

Chapter Two: The Middle

The move to this new house in a rural location was very upsetting for me! My mom had the house built, which meant it was a permanent home for us. I was very upset because I had to leave all my friends again. Not only did I have to leave my friends, but I had to attend a new school. I was starting middle school and that was a major change for me. We were in the county and there were not many people like me at this new school. I was terribly upset. But, the new house was nice. It was brand new--new flooring, new cabinets, a laundry room, one-and-half bathrooms, and a huge yard.

I didn't know what to expect at this new school. I remember walking into the school on my first day; I was horribly nervous. I found my homeroom, and when I walked in the kids stared at me. My teacher was clearly backwoods-country because she had a buzz cut across the top and the rest of her hair hung down her back. Aside from that, she didn't dress like a lady. She wore twill pants, a t-shirt, a huge jacket, and hiking boots. She was not what I expected at all. I remember one of her favorite sayings: "Don't sit there like a bump on a pickle!" It didn't make sense to me then and it still doesn't. I just figured she was country.

My seventh-grade year was weird. It was the year I started my menstrual cycle and I didn't know what it was. I thought I had done something wrong when it happened. I went home and told my mom. She told my sister, "Go up there to Gibson's (a department store) and get her some of those things." I had no clue what she was talking about. The day after starting my cycle, I was going to the bus and my mom yelled, "Did you get one of those things to take with you?" I politely said "Yes, mam." I lied. I didn't have any with me because she didn't tell me I had to take extra with me. I was kind of mad with my mom because she never told me anything about a menstrual cycle.

At school, we spent our mornings in the auditorium until the bell rang for first period. I was the new girl so I didn't know anyone. When I went into the auditorium, some of the guys were throwing around something gold. I looked because I was trying to figure out what it was, but didn't have a clue. So, I finally asked one of the guys what they were throwing and he said, "Condoms. You don't know what a condom is?" I said oh, ok. I was totally embarrassed because he proceeded to announce to everyone within ear shot that I didn't know what a condom was. Understand that this kid was probably 14 and in the seventh grade. So clearly, I was the smart one between the two of us. By the time we were nearing the end of the school year, I was comfortable with my new school. I started getting into trouble often because I wanted to fit in. Some of my classmates found out that my mom was a preacher, so I was teased a lot for being sanctified.

I started acting out because we never talked about my parent's divorce. I recall one incident where I went home and randomly lied to my mom. I made up some story about the principal--how when I was feeling sick, he wouldn't let me use the phone and I threw up on his desk. I was crying out for attention at the time. So, the next day unbeknownst to me, my mom decided to follow up with my little story. The next thing I knew, I was getting called to the office and there she was. My principal was sitting there looking at me crazy and my mom was surprisingly calm. I'm not sure what their conversation was before I went into his office, but I could only imagine. I thought my mom was going to beat me, but she only talked to me, hugged me, and went back to work. I'm sure my mom knew I was acting out because I wanted to get her attention. She never said anything else about it. I didn't do well in the seventh grade. I had to go to summer school for math so I could pass to the eighth grade.

When I started the eighth grade, I still had no boobs, no shape, but I had long hair. I loved my hair. Of course, back then most of us (me and my friends) had long, pretty hair. It was in the eighth grade that I started having more emotional problems. I don't think my mom knew what to do besides pray for me. I spent quite a bit of time crying at night, for reasons I didn't understand. My mom tried to soothe me, giving me warm milk and talking to me. I was keeping her up at night, but she was very patient about the situation. We spent a lot of time at church; going to revivals and two services every Sunday. I was singing with my mom and sisters during that time, but I was also struggling with being saved. My mom never knew it, but I was struggling with fitting in with my friends and living for God. I couldn't explain it to her because I didn't know what it was. It was like something was pulling at me all the time. I wanted to resist it, but I struggled to do so.

One day as we were nearing the end of the first semester of eighth grade, I sat in class, I took out a piece of paper, and started writing. On that paper, I wrote my new year's resolutions. I don't remember everything I wrote on the list, but I do remember the first thing I wrote was 'get saved' and there were a few more things on the list pertaining to going to church and being obedient. I kept the list for some time, carried it with me all the time, and then one day I decided to toss it. We were on break at school and when the bell rang to go back inside, I just threw it towards the garbage can and never looked back. Well, when I made it to my next class, my list was being passed around. One of the girls (who was a bully to me and didn't like me) had found it on the ground, read it, and was showing it to

7

everyone. My name wasn't on it, but I was totally humiliated. My classmates made jokes about it and they laughed. I just sat there and tried to ignore it. Because I didn't say anything, she accused me of having written it and I denied it. I went home that night and cried.

By the time eighth grade was over, I was in and out of trouble, my grades were minimal, and I spent a lot of time in detention. And yes, I had to go to summer school again. My dad had to pay for it and he was furious. I think it was during my middle school years that I realized I was different, and God had His hand on my life. I didn't understand it and I didn't know how to explain it to my mom. I think she felt bad because she didn't know how to help me; and my dad's way of helping was giving me money or taking me shopping. I was struggling to find myself which was evidenced by my low grades and failure to put forth my best efforts. I was crying out for help, but no one knew.

After middle school, it seemed like high school flew by. I had to go to summer school a few more times, but that seemed to be a running theme with me. In the ninth grade, I had developed boobs and some of the boys started calling me "three liter gallons." It was rude and I just laughed it off. I had made quite a few friends by then and I had settled in to going to school in the county. My mom was going to school to be a cosmetologist, so I had a different hairstyle every week. That resulted in the nick name "EnVogue." I laughed it off, but took it as a compliment. I was still being teased by the popular crowd because I was a preacher's kid and still a virgin. I struggled academically in school because I spent so much time day dreaming. My imagination was all over the place. I loved writing and I did well in English, but I failed to do as well in other classes. By the time of my tenth-grade year, most of my friends were pregnant and I was still being teased for being a square. I was getting into trouble, but not as much. I had detention and in school suspension a few times. My eleventh-grade year was a blur because my mom didn't let me do anything. I went to school, church, and home. She was strict; I can only recall going to maybe two football games. Besides that, I spent most of my time reading and writing in my diary. I was super happy in my senior year! I was finally getting ready to get away from my school and get some freedom from my mom. I was hanging out with the "in crowd" by the time I was a senior and I was glad not to be the recipient of as many jokes. My attitude was horrible though. I just didn't care and I was always getting smart with someone.

I enjoyed a few senior skip days and I did experiment with drinking a little; but nothing beyond that. By the time my last semester of my senior year started, I was sure I had everything I needed. One day I was called to the guidance counselor's office and she told me I had to pass all my classes or I wouldn't graduate because I would fall short a credit. I was upset because this lady waited until three months before graduation to tell me this. I was struggling in chemistry at the time and I was sure my chemistry teacher hated me. So, I went home and told my mom the news and she said to make sure that I passed chemistry so I could graduate. My dad had already spent hundreds of dollars on my senior portraits, my class ring, and customs invitations--not to mention my t-shirt, class mug, memory book, and whatever else I wanted.

I did what my mom told me to do: I spoke with my chemistry teacher and she told me to make sure to do all my homework, classwork, and turn in my notebook for extra points at the end of the year. I was struggling with a high F or borderline D in her class. If I could get a 70, I'd pass her class and graduate. Well, when it was all said and done, my chemistry teacher did not keep her word and I did not graduate with my class. I was devastated! I had already sent out invitations, made plans with my friends, and I was too embarrassed to call my Aunt/Uncle to tell them what happened. They came by the house the night of graduation and I explained it to them. My Aunt, who was a teacher, encouraged me and told me it was "okay."

After graduation was over, some of my friends came by the house and wanted to know what had happened. I told them and they wanted to know what could they do. They said "We will put sugar in her gas tank. You name it, we'll do it!" I was truly appreciative at that moment for good friends. They felt bad because I had helped a few of them when they needed it. We still hung out that night after graduation and it was great. The next day, reality set in that I had to complete a correspondence course from a local university to meet the required credits for graduation. My dad was livid, but he paid for it. I received the course work by mail and once I completed it, I mailed it back to the instructor at the university. The university sent me my grade and course credit, and also sent the information to the school. Once everything was completed, my mom told me to go to the school to pick up my diploma. So, I drove out to the school, walked into the office, and gave the secretary a copy of the information from the university. She took it and I asked for my diploma. She looked at me and said, "It's locked in the closet, I don't have a key, and I can't give it to you." I don't remember what I said, but I got in the car and I drove home crying. When I walked in the house, my mom asked what happened and I told her. She grabbed her purse and keys and said, "Let's go!" We went to the school; my mom walked into office and demanded the secretary to give me my diploma. My mom was so mad that she was about to go over the counter at her. This lady walked over to her desk, took out a key, unlocked the closet door, and gave my mom my diploma. I was shocked that a person could be so cruel to a child. My mom snatched my diploma from her and said, "I'm so sick of these white folks, I don't know what to do." My mom gave me my diploma and we left. I don't remember much of the conversation on the way home, but my mom was upset! She was fussing about how a person could be so lowdown and about how prejudiced they were at the school. I was officially a high school graduate, so it was time to get myself prepared for the next chapter of my life. It gets interesting from here.

Chapter Three: Experiencing Life

I attended college at a Historically Black College or University (HBCU). It was in state; my sister and cousin had gone before there me. It was about three hours from home, but that was enough for me. During my freshman year, I was roommates with a cousin on my dad's side. We hadn't seen each another since I had moved from our small hometown, so we were happy to reconnect with one another. I didn't know what to expect, but it worked out great. We both had the same major; she was there on a band/academic scholarship and somehow, I ended up on the flag line for the band. So, we went to breakfast, lunch, and dinner together. I was still adjusting and getting use to college life. We (freshman) were considered the 'crabs' of the campus. I met a guy who was a junior and he seemed nice. We were in the caf (cafeteria) and he walked up to me and said something random about my earrings. He also had hoops in his ears, which for some reason, I loved. I spent a lot of time with this guy the first semester of my freshman year. I was surprised because he was a junior and I didn't think he had an honest interest in me, but he did.

By the time the spring semester started, I was in a relationship with this guy, had moved out of the room with my cousin, and moved in with my friend from Chicago. At this point, I was getting my full college experience on. I went to all the parties and hung out with my guy and his fraternity brothers. I was drinking more and studying less. My drinking started getting out of hand because it was to the point that my cousins had to carry me to my room. Oh yes, I also started smoking marijuana. I was getting high with my home girls and college friends on a regular basis. That only contributed to my lack of studying and interest in going to class. As for my guy, the junior, he was still around. He waited for me at my dorm, my class, the library, or wherever I went. At some point, I started to get bored with him and ended the relationship. I don't know why because he was a nice guy; but I felt like he was a bit too much. I remember one Thursday, I went to the club with the rest of my girls; we had already smoked a few blunts, and I was having some drinks. Suddenly, my homeboy came in and insisted that I come outside. He was my ex boyfriend's fraternity brother. When I asked, "Why?" He said, "Come on home girl. I need to show you something." I was thinking, "This dude is seriously blowing my high!" But, I went outside anyway. I saw these people standing around a ditch. They were watching something or someone in the ditch. So, I proceeded to the middle where I could get a clear view and guess who was in the ditch? Yep, you guessed it; my ex had apparently fallen in the ditch because he was inebriated and calling my name. So, my home boy felt it would help him to see me. I don't know why he thought that was a good idea. I just felt sorry for him. At some point his fraternity brothers managed to pull him out of the ditch and take him to his dorm. I saw him some time later and he seemed embarrassed by the situation because he couldn't look at me. Meanwhile, my grades were suffering and the freshman year was winding down. I managed to make it through the last semester with a decent enough GPA to keep my financial aid and stay in school.

I went home for the summer, and pretty much did nothing! I had a group of friends whom I connected with and all we did pretty much was to go to the clubs and drank a lot of alcohol. I didn't date much in my home town because everyone dated in circles. I was not trying to connect with someone who probably had a history with someone I knew. So, the summer came to an end (thank God!) and I was on my way back to my HBCU to start my second year of college.

The sophomore year started with a back-to-school party. Of course, I was there. Some of my home girls with whom I had started college didn't return the second year for some reason, but I couldn't dwell on that. Although I enjoyed partying and drinking, I was determined to focus more on my grades so I could stay in school. I started the year doing well. My roommate was from my hometown, so we were getting along. It was during this year that she started dating a guy from a small town in the surrounding area. While she was dating him, I was kind of a third wheel to them.

I recall one time, my roommate was looking for her boyfriend so we decided to go to his hometown. She had a car and the town was so small we found his best friend's house. He was polite enough to invite us in and we waited for her boyfriend. He eventually arrived and we went to a 'hole-in-the-wall' club to party and have some drinks. While we were there, he introduced us to some of the locals who were his friends. We also met some of their friends from another town. I met for the first, the guy who was to become my boyfriend. We hit it off and from that point on, my roommate and I were hanging out off campus every weekend. The guy that I met was quite older than I was, but we had similar interests. We linked up every weekend at the club and we eventually exchanged numbers. Before long, my roommate and I were going to this club, not only on the weekend, but throughout the week. By this time, we'd met more friends and totally forgot about going to college. She had connected with a new guy since the relationship with the guy from college didn't work out. We were having the time of our lives--at least we thought so.

Meanwhile, my first cousin was going by my dorm room back on campus and eventually called and told my mom she hadn't seen me on campus in two weeks. At this point, I found myself in a relationship with the guy who seemed to be nice and

15

I was enjoying life. We liked freedom, drinking, getting high, and clubbing. As time progressed, my roommate and I decided not to go back to college. We decided we would get an apartment together along with another local girl. However, that wasn't so easy to do so. While we were looking for a place to live, we couch hopped; we lived from friend to friend.

One day, we were doing our typical thing: riding around looking for weed, and for something to eat and drink. We had some money, so we had gotten a hotel room. We were cozy--just hanging out in the room when there was a knock at the door. It was the police and we all scattered. I ran and hid in the shower (like they wouldn't find me) and, of course, they were looking for me. My dad had hired a private investigator and the rest is history. I was reunited with my dad and he was drove me home; yelling at me along the way. He had his gun and threatened to kill me, himself, before he would let me continue the life I was living. That had to be the longest car ride of my life. When I got home, my mom and sister were there waiting for me. It didn't take long for me to realize I didn't want to be at home. The next day, I learned my roommate's mom had found her and had picked her up as well. I called her after she came home and she said her mom had taken her car keys. She was on total lock down. She was still talking to her guy and I was still talking to mine; so, we decided we would go back to them. We decided to wait a few days before we left.

The day we left, I sat down and wrote my mom a long note about how I was grown and I wanted to live my life. She was at work, so by the time she got the note, I would be at my destination. We left a week after our parents picked us up and went right back to our guys. We were so excited to get back! We immediately connected with our friends and made plans for the night. We again, had no place to live, very little money, and were back to couch hopping. After being there some time, we were finally able to get our own place, along with another friend. We thought we had made it because our parents said we wouldn't. I had a job at a shoe store in the mall and both of my roommates worked. At night, we partied; I mean we partied hard! We frequented a local club that stayed open until 5:00 a.m.

I was still dating my guy and by this time, I thought we were serious. Well, he started to show his true colors; he started being abusive. At first, it was only verbal abuse, but it was on a regular basis. I was afraid of him and he would come visit me in his baby mother's car or she would call his phone while we were together. He would spend weekends with her and act like it was not a big deal. He was basically using both of us, but neither of us could see it at the time. I eventually stopped working at the shoe store in the mall and I started working at a restaurant. The hours were long, but the money was much better. I was paid every week and he would come pick me up, take me to the bank, tell me how much money to put in my account and how much I could keep. In my mind, this was an ideal relationship because, honestly, I didn't know what a real relationship was like.

Unfortunately, I continued to see him. When I wasn't working, I was smoking, drinking, and clubbing with him. By the way, he wasn't working so he had plenty of free time while I worked. There was one instance when I had to work; it was Father's Day and my birthday weekend. We all planned to go to the club and do our thing. However, I had to work later than everyone else, so my guy's brother (who treated me like a sister) said he would swing by and pick me up. We all agreed that was the plan. After work, I went home and got dressed. His brother came by to pick me up. At the club, we parked and my guy came out of the club, clearly upset. He looked at me, looked at his brother, and immediately started making accusations. He said "So you are f****** my brother now?" He then proceeded to throw me down on the hood of his brother's car and attempted to pull down my underwear to check for himself. His brother had to intervene and make him stop. I was totally caught off guard, but I gathered myself and went inside the club.

Once inside, he totally ignored me and then I saw his baby's mother. I thought to myself, "Really?" He had had her there with him the whole time, so he had to pick a fight with me to get the heat off him. I remember getting so drunk and partying all night. I had to be at work at like 5:30, so I literally left the club, went home, showered, and went to work. I was so drunk that I could hardly function. I made it through the day and went home.

When I got home, I washed my hair, combed it to the back because I had recently cut it very short, and I was sitting downstairs smoking a cigarette and drinking a beer. The next thing I knew, there was a knock at the door and in walked my guy. I immediately took off running and he caught me on the stairs. He was still angry--choking me and threatening to kill me if I ever disrespected him like that again. My roommate was screaming for him to stop and let me go, but he didn't do so until he was ready. He finally let me go and left.

I remember just sitting there thinking how tired I was: how so tired I was of him, the lifestyle I was living, and not being able to sleep at night. I had not been to church in forever and the devil was clearly trying to kill me. I just cried and my roommates sat around me saying that he was crazy and they wouldn't be with him. I thought I was in love, so I still didn't stop seeing him. Also, I didn't stop seeing him after those two incidents because I was afraid of him. But, eventually reality set in and I knew I had to leave before my parents would have to bury me. I didn't know when, but I knew I had to leave that place. I didn't belong there and I missed my family.

One day I was home alone and he came over again. We were sitting around and my pager beeped. Well, before I could get it, he jumped from the couch, grabbed it, and looked at the number. It was a Louisiana number--a number belonging to a guy at my job. It was nothing, but he was livid! He started cursing me; I put my beer down and walked upstairs to my bedroom. I sat on the bed and he followed me. He sat on the bed and asked me about the number and accused me of having sex with someone else again. I just looked at him. The next thing I know, he grabbed a pillow and he put it over my face. At first I tried to push the pillow off my face, but the more I tried to resist, the more pressure he added. Once I realized he was trying to kill me, I started saying the 23rd Psalm and stopped moving. At that point, he removed the pillow from my face and said, "The next time you do it; I'm going to kill your mother f******* a**!" Then he left.

When I heard his car go down the hill, I picked up the phone, called my dad collect and asked him to come pick me up. I knew I had to leave before he killed me. The next morning, my dad was there ready to help me pack. He couldn't get a moving truck on such short notice, so he rented a 15-passenger van. I didn't even care about the furniture, so we threw what we could in that van and left. I went by my job to pick up my check and told my boss I was leaving. He said that was the best thing for me because I didn't belong with those people I was hanging out with. Just like that, I was gone. I was so glad to be going home and getting away from the life I was living.

Once I got home, my mom welcomed me back and I settled into a routine. My dad told me, however, that I had to either get a job, go to the military, or go back to school. I was thinking to myself, "I'm not doing anything." So, for a while, that's what I did--absolutely nothing. Well, at some point my mom became fed up with me staying at her house, doing nothing all day, and eating her food; so, she called my dad. The next thing I knew, my dad was at my mom's house early one morning yelling for me to get up and get dressed. I asked, "Why?" He kept screaming for me to do it. I got up, showered, got dressed, and got in the car with him. I didn't know where we were going at first. Then I realized he was taking me back to school. I was so mad! We arrived at my college and he started asking me what I needed to do to get back in school. I wouldn't tell him anything. So, he asked the security guard where he had to go to get me in school. The security guard directed him to the registrar's office.

(I was cursing the security guard out in my head.) We got to the registrar's office and my dad walked in and asked, "What do I need to do to get my daughter back in school?" The worker asked for my social security number and I wouldn't say a word. My dad put his brief case on the counter and pulled out a copy of my social security card and gave it to her. She told him I had a balance that had to be paid before I could be cleared for registration. My dad said, "No problem, where do I pay it?" She pointed him in the direction of the business office. We went over to the business office; he paid the balance and got the receipt. We then went back to the registrar's office and I was cleared to enroll in school. We spent the whole day getting me back in school. When we were done, my dad told me I had until 2000 to finish school or he would cut me off. I was upset because I was still considered a freshman, I would be returning in the Spring of 1997 and that meant I would have to take 19 hours per semester and go to summer school. My dad was unbothered because he had given his final say.

I returned to school totally focused. I took 19 hours every semester, went to summer school and even joined a sorority in the spring 1998. I managed to get a job, qualify for work study, and stay on track to graduate. Even though I was focused, I started to enjoy being back on campus. I had a night class with one of my best friends and after that class we would sit in his truck, smoke a blunt, drink Hennessey and Alize' (also known as 'Thug Passion') and I would listen to him talk about how much he loved his girl, but she didn't trust him. I was his counselor, basically. His girl didn't like me or any other of his female friends. That's pretty much what I did on a regular basis. When I wasn't at work or in class, I was getting high or drinking. However, after I joined my sorority, I slowed down on the smoking and drinking. Besides, I had gained the freshman 15 pounds and then some. I started taking diet pills, signed up for a conditioning class, and started lifting weights. I went to summer school and continued to work my jobs. Before I knew it, I was a senior and I only needed about 15 hours to complete before graduation. The summer of my senior year, I convinced my dad to get me an apartment not far from campus. It was just a one-bedroom apartment, but it felt good to have a sense of independence. I was still hanging out with my best friend getting high and drinking 'thug passion' a few times a week. In June 1999, I was single and just hanging out with a guy from campus. He'd tried to talk to me a few times before, but he had a reputation around campus, so I hadn't given him much of my time. For some reason, we linked up while we were in summer school and he came over on my birthday. I'm sure I had more than my share of drinks and he did as well. We enjoyed that one night and the next month, I found out I was pregnant. I was devastated to say the least. I had plans for law school after graduation and a baby was not included in that plan. When I told, him I was pregnant, he said he wasn't the father because he used to see 'my boy's' truck at my apartment all the time. I explained to him that we were just friends getting high; but he didn't believe me. To make matters worse, I found out I was pregnant with twins and abortion was not an option. I cried because, at that time, I didn't want kids.

The fall semester started and the rumor mill was all over campus that I was pregnant with this guy's twins. My sorority sister was back on campus, so we decided we would go to the back-to-school party at the club. I told her I would come to campus and pick her up, but I had to do it quickly because I was avoiding a former boyfriend, D. I was avoiding him because I knew he'd heard I was pregnant and wanted to talk to me. But, I just couldn't face him—we had had a decent relationship. I rode on campus and the first person I saw was him. He spotted my car and I hit the gas trying to hurriedly pick up my sorority sister and get off campus. I managed to get her and we made it back to my apartment. As we were talking, getting caught up, and getting dressed to go out, there was a knock at my door. I asked, "Who is it?" He said. "D." I was shocked! I opened the door, he came in, and the conversation went like the following.

Him: "Hey. How you doing?"

Me: "I'm fine 'D'. How are you?"

Him: "I'm alright."

Me: "That's good."

Him: "I heard you're pregnant with twins by this guy, you're due March 23rd, and he's denying the babies are his."

Me: "Yes, that's true."

Him: "So, why don't we get back together, tell him the babies are mine, get married, give them my last name and I'll raise them as my own."

Me: "No, that's ok. I think he'll come around."

Him: (drops his head/stands up to leave) and says, "Okay, take care."

I walked him to the door and I never saw him again. My sorority sister, who was in my room listening, walked into the living room, looked at me and said: "B****, you are stupid! Old boy ain't going to do s***!" At that moment, I instantly regretted turning D down because I knew she was right. The semester went on and I learned my pregnancy was high-risk and I had to spend my last semester at home on bed rest. I completed my last courses through correspondence because of my circumstances. I had the twins via cesarean section in February 2000 and I graduated from college in May 2000. That was it; I'd accomplished what I set out to do--I had obtained my college degree. I thought life would get easier from there. Little did I know; my struggles were only beginning.

Chapter Four: Sacrificing Myself

When I graduated, I didn't receive my diploma because those are mailed. Well, I waited, and waited and I waited. My degree never arrived. I finally had to phone my college to find out what happened with my degree. I learned that my department chair failed to complete her paperwork as it pertained to my degree. So, I had to get my parents involved to help me with the situation. From that point, my dad was threatening to get a lawyer before my college finally came up with a solution. There was a new chairwoman in the English Department, and she was left to resolve the situation. It was just a blessing that my God sister was still in college there and she was so helpful in getting the paper work directly to the Chairwoman, as opposed to my mailing it off and hoping that she would get it. After some time and a few signatures later, I finally received my degree. It was truly a bittersweet day. It was just another testimony of my having to fight for and overcome the things that matter to me. A running theme seemed to be developing in my life.

I didn't know what I wanted to do with my life because I had had plans for law school until I found out I was pregnant. The jobs in my hometown were so limited; so, I eventually ended up working at a daycare and living in the projects not far from my job. It was at this stage of my life that I came across my old chemistry teacher from high school. I happened to be at the beauty salon and in she walked. I immediately recognized her and I hoped she didn't recognize me, but she did. The conversation went something like this:

Her: "Well, hello Ms. Porter."

Me: "Hello Mrs. …"

Her: "Do you forgive me?"

Me: "Yes, I do. The fact that I didn't graduate from high school motivated me even more to go to college."

Her: "Oh, really?"

Me: "Yes. I just graduated from college and I am preparing to go to graduate school."

Her: "Well, that's impressive, Ms. Porter. I'm very happy to hear that."

I felt vindicated at that moment because she thought not graduating from high school would stop me from going to college. I call people like her "dream killers."

During this time, I was trying to figure out what I wanted to do with my life. So, I applied to a university about 20 minutes from where I lived. I was still working at the day care in the meantime. One day my sister called me because she wanted to get the twins and to borrow my truck. I went to her house to pick her up on my lunch break. I put my son and my nieces in the truck and buckled them in their seats. I was waiting for my sister to come out; so, I stepped inside the house to tell her I had to get back to work because my break was almost over. I was gone not even one minute and my son managed to climb out of his car seat and pull the gear shift down. (I had an old 1992 Ford Explorer, four-wheel drive.) The next thing I knew the truck was rolling backwards with all the kids in the car and my son was jumping up with his hands in the air as if he were on a roller coaster. I quickly assessed the situation to figure out how to stop with truck. If I were not able to stop the truck, it would roll right into the neighbor's living room window, just a few feet from the street. I knew it was by God's grace that I could grab my niece who was walking to the truck as it was rolling, throw her under the steering wheel and throw the truck in park. By that time, my nieces were crying and I was such a nervous wreck that I could hardly calm down.

While the truck was in motion going down the driveway, I felt it roll over something. My sister insisted it was her foot but I wasn't sure. I saw that my daughter, who had come out the house during the commotion, was lying on the ground. I picked her up, assuming I had only knocked her down. I noticed a few minutes later that her breathing was terribly slow. It seemed as if she were struggling with each breath. My sister and I packed the kids in the truck and I went back to work. When I got to work and I explained to my supervisor what happened, she took one look at my daughter and said, "Take her to the emergency room, now!"

At that point, we were in a panic because we had no money and very little gas in the truck. We were afraid to go all the way across town to the hospital and possibly run out of gas on the way. So, we took her to a walk-in clinic initially, but were told they couldn't see her because she would need X-rays. My daughter's breathing was getting progressively worse and I had totally panicked at this point. When I returned to the truck where my sister waited with the other kids, I saw an ambulance right across the street. It was by the grace of God that the walk-in clinic was located right across from an ambulance service. I walked up to the ambulance and knocked on the door. I was near tears when the EMT opened the door. I explained to him what happened and he said we needed to get her to the hospital.

We finally arrived at the hospital and my daughter's vital signs were checked immediately. Based on her vitals, the doctor ordered an X-ray, which didn't reveal that anything was wrong. The doctor then ordered an MRI for further evaluation; the results showed my daughter had a lacerated liver. As I was told the news, I screamed and began to cry. I thought I was going to lose my child. The doctor on call at the ER called in a specialist for her case, who came in to explain the next steps in the process. The doctor said that surgery was not an option because the liver had the capacity to heal itself. He said she would need a catheter, an IV for fluids, heart monitor, and oxygen. She was the first child to ever be admitted in ICU at that hospital. After having gone through all of that, I watched various hospital personnel come in to poke and prod my daughter. During this whole process, she never said a word; she was traumatized from the accident.

While I had been sitting in the ER, I called my mom and my daughter's father. I also called my dad and a few other people. I was so afraid for my child and myself. While I was sitting and waiting, a lady walked in the room. She asked me if I were the mom and I said that I was. Then she introduced herself and explained that she was from Social Services. My heart sank! I thought they were going to take my child from me! I was sitting there crying and answering her questions, when in walked the doctor. He took one look at the social worker and immediately became upset. It went something like this:

Doctor: "What are you doing here?"

Social Worker: "I'm here to assess the situation involving the child."

Doctor: "The situation? This not a child who is neglected, mistreated, or abused. I've seen children who were such victims, and this child isn't! This child is well taken care of and is clearly a victim of a freak accident! There is no need to 'assess the situation' because it is not a situation! Who called you?"

Social Worker: "The EMT reported the situation and I had to follow up."

Doctor: "Well, the EMT was wrong!"

Social Worker: (Promptly gathered her things and left.)

The doctor turned to me and told me to calm down; he would take care of the situation. It was shortly after that that my daughter was admitted to ICU. I didn't sleep much because I was watching everything that was going on. My daughter had so many tubes coming from her body that it seemed unreal.

Sometime after midnight, her father finally arrived. His brother-in-law had driven him over two hours to the hospital. They were allowed in due to the situation, although ICU had visiting hours at a certain time. Once he arrived, he was not much help. He asked what happened and I told him. He said it was my fault and became angry. I told him it was his fault because in the past while he was driving, he had allowed our son to stand in his lap and hold the steering wheel. At some point, his brother in-law-told us that then was not the time for accusations. We agreed and stopped arguing.

His brother-in-law began asking questions that he should have been asking. I explained the prognosis and what the next steps were. Her father only said, "Okay." So, for a few minutes, there was an awkward silence, as we stood there watching our daughter. At some point, his brother-in-law said he had to leave and my daughter's father said he was leaving with him. His brother-in-law looked at him surprisingly and asked, "You're not staying?" He said, "Naw. I just wanted to check on her." His brother-in- law was clearly upset and he apologized to me on behalf of my daughter's father.

When they left, I sat in the chair beside my daughter's bed. I guess I dozed off because the next thing I remember is the nurse waking me up to speak with me. She told me that my daughter was bleeding internally and needed a blood transfusion. I immediately became upset and started crying. I didn't want to sign the permission papers because I was afraid the blood would be contaminated. The nurse assured me that extreme care is taken with donated blood and that my daughter badly needed the transfusion. I was hesitant, but I signed the permission form. I sat and watched my sleeping child, praying she would be alright. I was only able to get a few hours of sleep that night. Before I

27

knew it, it was 6:00 a.m. and I was still hoping my daughter would talk again.

I was sitting there watching cartoons; when the nurse came in to tell me that we had visitors. I looked up to see my cousin, my God mother, and a few co-workers with whom I'd previously worked at the local head start. They came to check on my daughter and to see if I needed anything. They couldn't stay long, but before they left, we stood in a circle around my daughter's bed to pray. It just so happened one of my former colleagues was a minister. He prayed a powerful prayer of healing for my daughter and peace for me. They weren't allowed to stay long, but an exception was made for their visit due to the extenuating circumstances. After they left, I turned the television to Tom and Jerry, in hopes of getting my daughter to talk. She was awake, but just lying in the bed sucking her lip. The next thing I knew, I heard the sweetest sound, "Mommy, look at Jerry; he's so funny!" I had tears and a smile at the same time. From that moment, she continued to make progress; getting stronger and eventually being moved to the children's floor in the hospital. A few days later, she was released with instructions for restricted movement (imagine that with a 3-year-old) and a two-week follow-up appointment.

After going through all that pain, I was totally focused on getting my life together. I continued to work at the daycare while I applied to graduate school, started going back to church, and I was determined to get myself together for my children. It was not the life I imagined after college, but at least I had some direction for what I wanted to do. I figured I would go to graduate school at a local college, major in rehabilitation counseling, get my license, and live on campus in family housing while doing so. I have learned over the years that the devil always had a plan to get me off course whenever I tried to live a life pleasing to God.

At about this time, I was living in my mom's house and I met a guy in the grocery store. We exchanged phone numbers and started communicating. He was a local minister from another town and I was not familiar with him. I was with my best friend at the time I met him, and he invited us to church. We went; only to learn that he was the pastor of the church. We were so tickled sitting in the back of that church while he was up there preaching. He was screaming like one of those old-school preachers. He and I started dating and sometime later, I learned I was pregnant. I was devastated. I couldn't phantom the idea of having another baby, working at a daycare, and trying to provide for all of them. I told him I was pregnant and decided I was going to have an abortion. He tried to talk me out of it the night before the appointment I had made to have it done. I pretty much forced my best friend to ride with me and drive me back. She was not in agreement with my decision, but I didn't want to hear her point of view either.

On the day of the abortion, we arrived early and it was like something out of a movie. There were protesters in front of the clinic with signs and they were screaming at everyone who went inside the clinic. I still didn't change my mind. Once we were inside, it was something to take in. There were teenagers, a very professional business woman, and single women like myself there. One young lady was visibly pregnant and looked to be about four or five months. That clinic performed procedures up to 24 weeks. I recall one mother who was there with her teenage daughter. The daughter had to be 14 or 15-years-old. The mother said they had driven four hours to get there. She said she didn't tell her husband and didn't want her daughter to be a teenage mother. After sitting there awhile, the professional lady dressed in the business suit went in before me and she took the "abortion pill," which would cause her uterus to contract and simultaneously extract the baby from her body later. I couldn't imagine being at home when that happened, but she seemed unbothered by it.

When it was my turn, they took me into a room, did an ultrasound to get an image, and explained to me what was about to happen. My best friend was with me and she begged me to look at the ultra sound, hoping that would change my mind. I refused. I was about six weeks pregnant, so the baby was about the size of a pea. The next sound I heard was something like a vacuum cleaner and within minutes; it was over. They took the bag with the remains of the baby out of the room, and gave me a maxi pad and I went to the bathroom. I came out of the bathroom, I went in the back to the recovery area where I had to stay for some time before being released to go home. I was still sedated when we left and my best friend drove us home. Once we made it back to town, she went home and I had to drive myself back to my home. I was still sleepy, but I could get home safely. I slept the rest of the day.

The next day I went to work; after I arrived home, later that evening the baby's father arrived. He came in the house and he seemed as if he were bothered. I was standing in the dining room and he just looked at me and said, "I can't believe you killed my baby." I was over it by this time and I explained to him that I couldn't afford another baby. The next thing I know, he threw me against the door in the dining room and begin to bang my head against the door several times. At some point, he stopped banging my head and as I was just barley standing he began to hit me several times. He was literally boxing me like I was man. I don't remember how long that lasted, but at some point, I tried to get away by running down the hall to lock myself in a room. As I was doing so, he caught me and threw me in the closet at the end of the hallway, causing the entire closet to completely detach from the frame of the house. After it was over, he sat in the living room chair as if nothing had happened.

I didn't know what to do. I was traumatized over the whole situation and he didn't leave the house. He just sat in the chair looking crazy, dazed, and confused. I was afraid, but I still tried to talk to him. I don't remember what happened the rest of the night, but the next day I filed charges against him and I called my dad. Of course, while my dad was at my house, he came over and my dad threatened him. I don't know why I had expected more from my dad considering he had done the same thing to my mom.

Even after that situation, I continued to see him and guess what? I found myself pregnant again. I knew I didn't have a choice but to keep it. The twins were four-year-old at the time; I had moved in the projects and was getting ready to start graduate school. I was so embarrassed by my pregnancy that I hid it as much as I could. I didn't tell my dad, but the word got out in my small hometown and it wasn't long before my dad found out. He was furious. He cursed me out; I don't remember what he said because I was in the third trimester of my pregnancy. Of course, one of the members of the baby father's church told my dad; I later found out she just happened to be my cousin. I had my baby in March and that's when the drama started. The church members came by my house and they wanted to see the baby. I was respectful to them and let them see her and they all said, "She looks just like Pastor." I was over it.

I started graduate school at a local university; but after I had my baby, I fell behind in my work. It was helpful for me that the university had a program where I could start over due to my extenuating circumstances. I did get a fresh start, but ultimately had to withdraw because it became a struggle driving back and forth and having to find babysitters for three small children a few nights a week. A friend of mine, who was also in graduate school, suggested I apply to an online program in which she was enrolled. She assured me it was totally legitimate and accredited.

After checking the program out, I applied and I was accepted. I was so excited.

At the time, I was working two jobs and completing my assignments at night while my children slept. I completed my graduate program in exactly one year and graduated the next year after taking my comprehensive examination. I was so excited. I was so proud because not only did I work two jobs, but I graduated with a 3.6 GPA, and I had my M.S.C.E. in Counseling/ Psychology. I can't put in words how excited I was.

The next step for me was to find a job and leave Mississippi; at least that was the plan. It didn't happen that easily though. I applied for several jobs to no avail. I finally decided maybe it wasn't time for me to leave Mississippi just yet. My cousin was employed with MSU and encouraged me to apply for a job similar to what she was doing. I applied and was interviewed. The interview went well and I was asked to come back for a second interview. While I was preparing for my second interview, I received a phone call from a mental health agency that was about an-hour- and-a-half away from Columbus. I went in for the interview and within a few days, I was offered the position. I decided to accept that job in Meridian because it was in my field. I went back to look for an apartment that was suitable for me and my kids. The next few weeks went by very quickly, as I packed up to leave my hometown. I was excited to finally have a fresh start; a new beginning away from all the drama; at least that was what I thought.

Chapter Five: Finding Myself

I had finished graduate school, earned my Master's degree, and I was on my way to Meridian, MS, to start my first job after graduate school. I was super excited, not only about the job, but about the chance to have a fresh start. My dad helped me to move and I think he was even more excited than I was. My apartment complex was amazing to say the least. It was on the North side of town; right off the highway and it had all the amenities, including a swimming pool. The kids were excited about that. These types of accommodations were things I was not use to because I had lived in two different public housing units after college. I truly felt like my life was turning around. I promised myself that once I was settled, I would find a church home. I was going to focus on my family and my career. That was my plan.

First, I had to find Lydia, my youngest daughter, a daycare and get the twins enrolled in an after-school program. That was truly an adjustment for me because back home, I had depended on my family for help with the kids. The daycare bill, combined with after school care, was so expensive! But I needed those services, so there was nothing I could do about it. After getting them all enrolled in school, I started my new job. I was employed at a local mental health agency as a mental health therapist/day treatment specialist. The first week on my new job was all orientation. I was in a room with other new hires and we went over all the policies, completed paperwork, and listened to members of the administration team speak to us. It was so long and boring, but was useful information. I was excited to start the next week because I was finally going to interact with my colleagues and start working in my capacity as a therapist. I had my own office and phone, and it all seemed surreal. I was assigned to several schools in the district, so I had to learn my way around the city.

After a few months or so of getting adjusted and becoming familiar with my job, I finally felt comfortable in my new surroundings. I was at work one day and I mentioned to one of the ladies who worked at the school that I was new to town and looking for a church home. She invited me to her church and informed me of their service times on Sunday and of weekly bible study. I was not able to make it to the Sunday service, so my first service was Wednesday night bible study. I remember the message so vividly because the title was, 'Answer the Call.' I enjoyed the service and everyone was so welcoming, but more than anything, the place seemed so familiar to me. I couldn't figure out why there was a familiarity at the time, but I knew I would join that church. After bible study, my friend introduced me to another young lady and she welcomed me as well. We exchanged pleasantries, and she asked if she could she share something with me. I told her yes and she proceeded to prophesy to me. She told me that the message was prophetically for me because the Lord had a call on my life. She told me it wasn't by accident that I came to the church that night. I received the word because I knew she was telling the truth.

Before I moved, I had been told by two other pastors that I had a call on my life. It's not that I didn't receive it; I just didn't know what to do about it. I didn't know what I was called to do. Was I called to preach, sing, or what? I had no clue as to what the Lord wanted me to do, but He kept reminding me about the call on my life. I went to church that following Sunday and I met the pastors of the church for the first time. They were truly amazing people. After service, the first lady walked up to me and said something I will never forget. She said to me "What are you waiting on daughter? You know what God said." I knew exactly what she was talking about, but again I didn't know what I was supposed to do about the 'call' on my life. The next Sunday, I finally joined the church and I was excited about what God was going to do in my life. I felt like my life was coming together and I was getting on track.

Outside of church, I wasn't involved in much of anything. I became good friends with the lady who prophesied to me when I first visited the church. She became a mentor to me, in addition to a lady with whom I worked at the school. The kids were settled in and doing well. I was still doing therapy and working in classrooms in schools throughout the district. I was assigned to a middle school, where I worked in the alternative classroom. In this room was Mr. M. He was newly married, seemingly a hopeless romantic, and insisted that I needed to date. I told him I wasn't interested, but he continued to say that Mr. T would be great for me. I insisted that I wasn't interested, but Mr. M had already purposed this in his mind. I used one of the offices in the school and I was in there when Mr. T knocked on the door with one of my clients. He was smiling from ear-to-ear. I thanked him for bringing my client down and proceeded with my session. After I sent the student on his way, I sat in the office and wrote notes. The next few days were spent introducing myself to the administrators, and meeting teachers and parents. I had such a huge caseload; it was imperative that I kept my work organized. As I was sitting one day in between sessions, there was a knock at the door. It was Mr. T and he was smiling. He was well dressed, tall, and clean cut. He came in ready to talk. We exchanged pleasantries and he just continued to talk. Before long, it was time for me to go. I told him I was not interested in dating, but this man would not take no for answer. He started coming by my little office every day and he offered to be of assistance in some capacity. The school was huge, so most days I agreed to let him get my clients out of class for me. Some time went by, and I found myself dating this guy. I will be honest; I was not attracted to him. I tried to tell him that but I wasn't clear. Before I knew it, about some 15 months had gone by and I found myself stuck in a relationship with this guy.

Over the course of those 15 months, so many things happened that I didn't plan. This guy was clearly a distraction to get me off God's plan for me. I allowed him to totally shift my focus; all because I didn't want to hurt his feelings. I started missing church and I was sharing with my friend at work one day how I was so tired of him and the whole situation. She looked at me and said, "Leda, you compliment him." She said it in such a nice way that it took me awhile to catch it. He was always buying me things: purses, shoes, jewelry and rings. The first ring he gave me was a platinum and diamond ring with baguettes on the side (I thought). That was my dream ring, so everything I ever said to him was void after he gave me that ring. After that, came the tennis bracelet with the matching ring, then the custom white gold and diamond wedding band. I was so blinded by those "things" at the time, I couldn't see how the relationship was holding me hostage.

Within those 15 months, I was presented an opportunity to teach sixth and seventh grades. I was the new alternative teacher. I was excited about the new employment opportunity and I had no doubt I would be successful. I remember the first day I wore my rings so proudly and I saw this guy. He caught my attention because he was fine. I'm just being honest. Anyway, time went on and I was adjusting to my new job and getting familiar with my expectations. I learned that my cousin was also employed at the school and lived in the city, too. We were excited because we hadn't seen each other in years. I felt instant relief because I had a family member near. It was so great for us to reconnect and get to know each other again.

The school year went on and by the spring semester, I was acclimated to my job. I had become acquainted with my colleagues and my principal was pleased with my work. Mr. T was still around getting on all my nerves. He started showing up at my job on his break because he was supposedly checking on his son who was a student there. What I later learned was he had been told that Mr. Fine was coming by my class, so he was there to spy on me. The "relationship" was slowly coming to an end and I didn't care anymore.

By the time the summer came around I was over the whole situation. I just wanted to be left alone. I was still dealing with Mr. T and he just didn't get it. I was still distracted from God's purpose for my life and I was missing church off and on. I missed one Sunday and my friend called me to relay a message from my pastor. He told her to tell me, "T is not God." I just started crying. I told her I was so tired, but I felt trapped. This man would not leave me alone. She encouraged me and said she would be praying for me. I can honestly tell you now, looking back on the whole situation, the devil had me totally distracted. I started praying more and asking God to reveal things to me about the relationship. I knew it was not His will for me. Mr. T even went so far as to show up at my church one Sunday, sat in the back with a ring (another one), and said he came there to propose marriage. My pastor saw him and he wanted to meet him. Hesitantly, I introduced him and the look on my pastor's face was priceless. I don't think he was what he'd imagined. I was somewhat embarrassed by the whole situation.

The summer was pretty much over and my kids had returned home from vacation. They were excited to be home and wanted to camp out in the living room and watch movies. I moved the furniture, put the comforters down and gave them a snack. I sat there with them for a while before going to my room to lie down. I was extremely tired for some reason, so I went to sleep not long afterwards.

This nap was not my typical nap. As I was getting into deep sleep, I was suddenly awakened, but I wasn't in my room anymore. My soul was detached from my physical body and I thought I had died. I looked and I saw people wearing hooded robes (my best description) pushing a large crank. They were just going in a circle, not saying a word. When I saw that, I thought about my kids and I said, "Oh, Jesus!" and before I knew it, I was back in my apartment on my bed. I jumped up from my bed to check on my kids and they had fallen asleep watching their movies. After I made sure they were alright, I went back to my room. I just began to cry. For the first time, I heard the voice of the Lord. The Lord told me to get on my knees and pray. I fell on my knees and through tears, I told the Lord, "I don't know what to pray." The Lord led me to my bible to read Joshua 1:5-9 and the covenant was established. After reading that passage, I began to speak in tongues. I was filled with the Holy Ghost in my home. God saved my life.

After having that experience, I didn't know what to think. I was still in shock over the whole experience. I never imagined something like that could happen to me. I called the next day to make an appointment with my pastor. I needed to tell him what I experienced and get his feedback. In the meantime, I called my mom to tell her what happened. She told me I had an out-of-body experience and people who have those experiences are special to the Lord. I was totally taken aback. I was still trying to understand why it happened to me. I knew it was a reason and for the most part, I felt God was trying to get my attention. I finally could meet with my pastor a few days later, and I shared my experience with him. He said to me, "Daughter, the Lord is showing you what can happen when you are in bondage." It was like a light bulb went off in my head! I knew the 'relationship' that I was so desperately trying to get out of was leading me to a place of bondage. I had become so caught up with him that it was causing me not to focus on my relationship with God. I was not out unless I was with him, I didn't go to church if we had an issue, and it was a struggle for me to have any kind of peace. While my heart truly desired to live a life that was pleasing to God, I struggled to do so. I knew from that moment on, I had to make a change. I had to commit myself fully to God.

The first thing I did was get rid of all things related to that relationship. If I kept his gifts, I would still have a connection to him. I had so much stuff that had to go. There were purses, shoes, clothes, rings, and bracelets-- just to name a few. I started with throwing away cards, and then I let the Lord lead me in giving away the things Mr. T had given me. I gave my purses to a few women in my church; I blessed my friend with the jewelry; and I gave the Coach travel bag to another good friend of mine. All of it was gone; it was finally out of my house. There was no more attachment to him. It wasn't so easy to get rid of him, but eventually I did. I told him I was pretty much done and he just couldn't handle it. He started leaving things at my door. At first it was just a card with a letter enclosed. When I didn't respond to that; he left roses at my apartment door; and when I didn't respond to that; he left more roses and about ten balloons at my door. I was so over it. The only difficult part about the situation was working with him in some capacity every day. I started getting phone calls from some random woman telling me she was in love with him and staying at his house every weekend or he was staying with her. I was so tired of it all. In the community, this guy was 'stand-up'; he was loved by all who interacted with him and he went above and beyond for the kids in the community and on his job. He seemingly was the perfect guy. But, I knew the truth. I also learned I didn't know him. He was basically a facade of what he presented himself to be. I told him to tell his girlfriend to stop calling my phone, but he denied it. It seemed the more I rejected him, the more he would try to hold on to me. There were a few times where I almost fell for his line again, but he would do something to remind me of why I had wanted to end the relationship initially. He started lying and disappearing again. I remember one night, I fell asleep and I had this very vivid dream. The dream was about him; he was at my apartment and we were watching television. While he was there, someone knocked on the door. I opened the door to find a lady who was very pregnant. She proceeded to tell me who she was and that the baby she was carrying was his. In the dream, he became a black figure, (something like a shadow or dark spirit) and he started jumping around, moving about all the while denying all the things the lady was saying. In the dream, I couldn't see the woman's face, but I could see her from the neck down. During the dream, a bright light suddenly appeared and it was my choir director, who was also my close friend. She appeared almost like an angel and she repeatedly said to me, "Seek truth." After that, I woke up. I felt like God was telling me something, but I wasn't sure. So, I started praying for God to remove him from my life and to reveal anything that was done in the dark.

After some time, I was finally able to get him out of my life. We worked at the same school, so our only interaction was there. He would try to text, call, or whatever, but I was not interested at all. One Sunday in January 2010, was family and friends' day at church. I'd invited one of my former students who had become like a son to me, and a colleague who was a good friend. As we were sitting in church, I noticed a woman sitting in front of me with a baby. I looked at the baby and I thought it was odd for the lady to have the baby lying on her shoulder sleeping. It looked as if the baby was uncomfortable to me.

I had to go sing with the choir and I came back to my seat. When I sat down, my friend tapped me on my leg and I as I leaned over, she whispered to me, "That's T's baby." I leaned my head to the side, got a good look at the baby and I looked over at my friend and said, "It sure is! She looks just like him!" Then I said to my friend, "That's why she won't lay the baby down, she wants me to see her!" I was floored because this woman came to my church and ended up sitting directly in front of me. I later learned her aunt was a member of my church and their family was not pleased about the whole situation with him and her. He apparently had used her and gotten her into some type of trouble. I did tell him I saw the baby and asked him about it; he still denied it. It didn't even matter. I just wanted him to be a man and admit what he'd done. But, he didn't and that was it. I was so glad it was over and I was no longer attached to that man in any way.

I spent almost four years living in Meridian. At the end of the 2009-2010 school year, I learned that because of budget cuts and the fact that I was a new teacher, my contract was not being renewed. I was devastated not knowing what to do. I applied for several jobs locally to no avail. I knew I had to go back home. I reached out to a friend of mine who was a supervisor for an agency in Tupelo at the time. She advised that she had no available jobs, but another program within the agency was hiring. I applied for the job and patiently waited to hear something. Meanwhile, the school year ended and we had potluck on the last day at the school where I taught. Of course, Mr. T was there and he stopped me to ask if we could talk. I thought he might finally tell some truth, so I said yes. We sat outside the teacher's lounge and he started off with an apology about everything. He still denied the baby, and claimed the lady had always liked him and that was why she lied on him. He also denied knowing the lady who was calling my phone; said he didn't know how she got my number. He said I had hurt him because I was talking to my friend, the Mr. Fine. I told him we were only friends and whatever happened between Mr. Fine and me happened after I left him. He then proceeded to talk about another guy with whom I had dated for a while and how that hurt him. I was not interested in providing him any feedback about who I may or may not have dated after I left him because that was not his business. Besides, I was leaving in a few weeks and I certainly wasn't going to miss him. I had an interview for the job I'd applied for and until I found a job, I had to temporarily move in with my mom. I never imagined going home again in this capacity--jobless, no place to call my own, very little money, and my three babies. I just had to trust that God had a plan, even when I didn't.

Chapter Six: Going Home Again

My contract was not renewed and I was not able to find a job so that I could stay in Meridian. God was letting me know my time in Meridian was up. I had an interview in Tupelo, which was closer to my hometown and my family. In the meantime, the plan was to stay with my mom. I went home for the interview and about 30 minutes later, I received a phone call from the Regional Director offering me the job. I gladly accepted the job. I finally felt like my situation was starting to work out. The following weekend I moved out of my apartment in Meridian, put my furniture in storage in Columbus, and moved in with my mom temporarily. Within three weeks, I had found a duplex to rent not far from my job. I was super excited! I was hoping Tupelo would be good for my kids and me.

I moved into my apartment with my kids' right before school started in Tupelo. My kids were growing up and I was eager to get them settled into their new environment. I was excited about my job; but I must admit I was not thrilled about being so close to home. I wanted to leave Mississippi, but that door wasn't opened for me to do so at the time. I just decided I would wait on God and let Him work things out for me. After getting settled in the apartment, the kids and I got in a routine of going to work and school. I was struggling with health issues involving hypertension and being overweight. The school year went by and before I knew it, the twins were graduating fifth grade and my baby was completing her first-grade school year.

It was during this time that I started to have issues related to my weight and just being unhealthy. I knew there was a significant history with my weight, but I had stopped trying to take care of myself while I focused on finding a job and providing for my kids. I didn't realize how much weight I'd gained until I saw a picture my dad took of me and the kids at their fifth-grade graduation. I was devastated! I knew I had to do something to get on track. At some point, I went to the doctor for a checkup, and some blood work was done. The results came in and all my numbers were slightly elevated. My blood pressure was high the day I went in for the appointment. I was advised to eliminate salt from my diet, eat healthy, and exercise 30 minutes a day. I didn't know how I was going to do that, but I knew my health depended on it. My doctor wanted to see me back in one month for a follow-up. In the meantime, I had to put forth some serious effort to take control of my health. I will admit during that time, I was adjusting to a new city, dealing with my emotions, and trying to get settled. There were times that I was eating because I was bored, so that contributed to my poor health. I loved to eat out and I especially loved pasta. Those were some habits I struggled to let go. Well, before I knew it, it was time for me to go back to the doctor for my follow-up. I went the day before my appointment to get my lab work done. The Dr. was not happy the next day when I saw her. She looked at me and said, "Ms. Porter, your numbers are still significantly high. If you don't make the changes, I'm going to put you on cholesterol medicine." I was devastated! I sat there and I began to cry. My lab work revealed that my cholesterol level was up, my blood pressure was elevated, and my I had gained a few more pounds-- all in one month! My doctor didn't change or add any medication to my current prescription, but she gave me information on a diet plan and stressed the need to incorporate exercise in my life. When I left the doctor's office, I went to join a local weight loss program and after that, I joined a gym. I prayed and decided I was going to focus on my relationship with the Lord, my family, and getting my health together. I had given too much of energy and time to failed relationships and my emotions. I was clearly doing more harm than good, and it was time to stop being careless!

I made needed changes. I had been living in Tupelo for over a year, my health was improving, my kids were doing great, and my job was going well. I decided to focus on my family and establish my career. I was so over relationships and I prayed that in due time the Lord would allow my husband to find me. I was content with myself and life was good.

One day at work, I walked in my supervisor's office at work to give her something and she was amid an interview. I apologized for interrupting her, but I still gave her what she needed. Before I left she asked me to give the candidate an idea of what he could expect if he were hired. I gave my little spill about the job and I left. I never thought anything else about it. Later that day, I learned the guy who was interviewed was a friend of one of my colleagues.

About a week or so went by and some of my colleagues in the office planned to go out the upcoming Friday to hang out and have drinks. I declined to go because that was not my thing; I did my drinking at home after my kids went to sleep. My colleague, with whom I'd never had a conversation, asked me repeatedly to come hang out. I continued to say no. After I turned him down, he had my case manager (with whom he had become very close) to try to get me to come. I was close with my case manager, but I told her "no" as well. I told her my kids and I watched movies and ate pizza on Friday. She said, "Come on LeLe! Please?" At some point, I finally gave in and agreed to go. I knew I was going to regret it later. They all seemed excited that I was coming. My colleague said, "My boy is coming." I said, "Ok." I just assumed he had gotten the job. I continued to talk with my case manager and my other colleague, who said, "He's coming to see you. You know that, right?" I looked at him and I said, "Oh, ok." I was not even slightly interested in his statement. So, Friday came and everyone in the office was excited about the employee outing that night. I didn't see what all the excitement was about, so I went about my day. After work I picked up my kids, got the pizza, and the movie they would watch. Once they were settled, I considered not going out with my colleagues. I guess my case manager must have known I what I was thinking because she called me to confirm that I was still coming. I hesitantly told her yes. I proceeded to get dressed and leave. I was the first to arrive at the restaurant, and then my case manager showed up. She also had another colleague with her and it was clear she had had one too many drinks. While we stood around outside talking and waiting for everyone else to show up, the girls started telling me how the new guy liked me and that's why he was coming to hang out with us. I told them I don't like guys with bald heads and they looked at me like I was crazy. I didn't apologize for it; I shrugged and told them that's my preference.

We all walked in the restaurant and I found our table. I was starting to have a good time, and it was good to get out for a little while. They were having a drink and I was drinking water, which everyone found to be humorous. I was still on my diet, so I didn't want to get off track. I ordered my food and was sitting there waiting; the new guy made his way down to where I was sitting. He initially didn't say much, but I started laughing at something my colleague said and he said, "Man, you have a beautiful smile." I politely said, "Thank you." That was the beginning of the conversation. I decided to be nice because I was not at all interested in getting to know this guy or his bald head. In my mind, I thought I'd play nice just to get me through the night. However, peer pressure, even as an adult, can be intense. So, at the end of the evening when I was getting ready to go home, my friends begged me to come with them. Apparently, the

46

new guy and our other colleague had gotten a room and everyone was about to hang out. I was so not interested in doing that, but again the peer pressure was intense. Reluctantly, I went and I was bored out of my mind! The new guy was continuously talking to me (making small talk) and I was about ready to go home. Eventually I got ready to leave and he walked me out. Once we were outside, he asked me to go for a ride. So, we hopped in this truck, literally rode a few miles up the street, chatted for a few minutes, and he took me back to my car. I was so glad that night was over.

I believe it was the following Monday at work that I learned the new guy would be sharing an office with me. I believe we exchanged numbers; but my plan was not to respond as he'd like and, hopefully, he would leave me alone. Well, that plan didn't work. He was persistent in his pursuit of me and it didn't help that I would see him at some point throughout my day. I honestly didn't know what to expect. At some point, our communication started to increase and we went out a few times. He was presenting himself as a nice guy, seemingly caring and genuine. In my mind, I thought I'd met the right guy, despite the bald head. I did have some concern because we were co-workers and we shared an office. I was not looking for another relationship, but I found myself in one with this bald guy. It was not a secret around the office and most days I felt embarrassed about the whole situation. If we were having an issue, it was a struggle being around him and trying not to exude that negative energy. As time went on, I learned to leave all of that outside work and focus on my job. He was still being nice, cooking for me, surprising me with gifts, going on trips with me, and taking me shopping. I knew it was all happening way too fast and he was too good to be true.

Chapter Seven: Disobeying God

A few months had gone by and I continued in the relationship. I think he really "hooked" me when my car broke down on me suddenly, ended up with over a thousand dollars' worth of repairs, and our supervisor would not work with me until I was able to pay for the car. He took it upon himself, went online, found me a car, and put the down payment on it. I never had any man, not even my dad, do that for me. In my mind, it seemed that during my most difficult times, he was a great support. We started spending more time together and by now our kids were involved. He lived about 60 or so miles from me, so our weekends were split in between our homes. By the time the New Year came around, we were discussing marriage and making plans for me and my kids to move in with him. This was something I never imagined doing until I was married; but I figured it would be alright. I spent months literally trying to convince myself that I could move in with this man who was not my husband. I told my mom, who was livid and encouraged me not to do it. Her exact words were, "We don't believe in shacking." He found it all hilarious; meanwhile, I was struggling. I prayed about it and I felt that it was fine. I proceeded with my plans to move; gave my landlords notice, and reserved a rental truck. The school year came to an end for my kids, and I started packing. It was all happening so fast.

Before I knew it, the summer was slowly coming to an end and it was time to move. I was packing my kitchen and praying about the move I was getting ready to make. I decided I would ask God again if this man were the one had He destined for me. So, I did and just as clear as a glass, I heard the voice of the Lord say, "No." I stopped in the middle of the kitchen and I just stood there. I knew I had to be obedient, but at that moment I started to rationalize with God. I started by saying, "But God, He is my husband." "We're getting married in a few months. He's my soul mate." I was still trying to convince God and myself that I was doing the right thing. Nevertheless, I continued to pack and within hours, we were loading the truck and moving to our new home. After we arrived, it was chaotic because we had to unload the truck and figure things out. We didn't think about how much we had together, so I stored some of my things and gave the rest to my mom. After everyone left, there was still so much to do. I continued to work until I couldn't anymore. I was trying to get as settled as possible and make my kids feel comfortable. On our first night in the home, he sat us down in the living room to give the kids what I thought would be a welcoming sort of speech. Instead, he cursed at the kids and I sat there in disbelief. My anxiety level was on 100. I couldn't eat anything without getting sick and my heart was beating rapidly. It was at that moment, I knew I'd made the biggest mistake of my life. He was this super nice guy, but once we were all under one roof, he turned into someone I didn't know. Basically, he started being himself.

The second day in the house was not better. My kids were gone with my family and I was just a wreck emotionally. I became upset because I wanted to leave. I wanted to go back to my duplex apartment with my kids and wait on the Lord. I could finally see I'd made the worst mistake of my life. As I sat in the chair crying, he was cursing and going on. I had fixed a sandwich right before he came in yelling and I couldn't eat it. I just sat there crying. I said very little because I was afraid of the person I was seeing. About an hour or so went by and I was still crying. He walked to the back of the house for a while and came back a few minutes later, sat on the love seat, and asked me to come over. He began to tell me how much he wanted me there and how much he loved me. I started to calm down and I thought things would get better. Boy was I wrong!

I moved in with my supposed fiancé' in July and we were supposed to get married a few months later. A few months turned into a whole bunch of excuses from him. I was cooking, cleaning, being a step mother, and everything else I felt the need to do as the woman of the house. I started gaining weight because I was drinking daily after work. He was so controlling that I didn't do anything. My cousins lived in the area, but I was not able to hang out with them as I wanted. He introduced me to his family and friends, but it meant nothing to me. He kept me drunk most of the time or he was coming home drunk. It was not an ideal situation for me and my kids. By the time Thanksgiving came around, I was miserable but I didn't show it. I wasn't sleeping much at night because of anxiety and I started trying new recipes as a coping mechanism. At this point in the relationship, it was a struggle for us because we were having disagreements over just about anything. I felt stuck because I had nowhere to go. I didn't know what to do. We spent Thanksgiving with my family and I put on the "happy face" and pretended all was well. After that, it started to go downhill. The Lord was dealing with me so heavily about being in that situation that I couldn't sleep at night. I prayed every night, asking for forgiveness and begging the Lord not to let me die in my sin. I kept telling God I wanted a way out, but I didn't know how to get out. So, I just continued to stay there. I kept going along, day-to-day, and I was miserable. He cursed me out, called me a female dog, a slut, or whatever else he felt the need to do in order validate his authority in the house.

With each passing day, our situation worsened. He began to sleep on the couch; I started sleeping in workout pants, t-shirts, and socks. Some nights I slept on the couch. I didn't sleep many nights because I was just unhappy, but I couldn't figure a way out. I continued to pray and ask God what to do. I was at a point of misery and I couldn't tell anyone. Well, I was too embarrassed to tell anyone that my seemingly 'happily ever after' was like living in hell. I was so broken down from verbal abuse that I was numb. I was self-medicating with alcohol and just falling apart all together. The holiday season was upon us and we were somewhat cordial to one another. I typically had to feel him out so I could determine how the rest of the evening would go after we arrived from work. By now it was December and call me crazy, but even though we weren't getting along, I thought for sure I would get my official engagement ring for Christmas. I was excited about the possibility, especially since we looked at rings. But that excitement was short lived. It was a few weeks before Christmas and he managed to finally tell me that I had to wait because he had taken out a loan to help with his daughter. I was not mad about that, I just felt deceived. I was hurt that I had been made a last priority once again. It was at that moment that I was done. I knew I had to leave, but I didn't know how.

On Christmas day, I decided to go over to my mom's and eat dinner with my family. He was upset because I initially agreed we would stay home and eat. After he went back on his word about the ring and the marriage, I just didn't want to be around him. He was furious. So, I packed up my kids and we drove to my mom's house. When I arrived, I tried to put on a happy face, but it was impossible to maintain that demeanor. As we prepared to eat, my family stood around the table while my mom blessed the food and I didn't join them. I sat in the living room almost in a state of shock. My mom motioned for me to come to the table and I refused. When they started eating, I walked to the back room of my mom's house and I broke down and cried. I couldn't hold it in anymore. I cried so hard that I could not breath. My mom walked in the room and she didn't ask me anything, but she knew. She simply consoled me and said, "Leda, the bible says don't be weary in well doing." She just continued to repeat that to me. I shook my head and said, "Mom, I tired. I'm so tired." My mom asked, "What are you going to do?" I said, "I'm going to leave him." She said, "I don't know Leda. It's going to be hard to leave him because that man loves you." I said "I don't care, I'm leaving. I can't take it anymore."

I left my mom's house Christmas day with my mind made up to leave him. I planned to leave as quickly as possible, but I found myself delayed. We managed to make it through the month of December in a somewhat peaceful manner, but after the New Year, we had a huge argument. It was so terrible that he again cursed me out, didn't shave or cut his hair for a few weeks, and disrespected me as usual. He did whatever he could to belittle me, even telling me that no one else would want me because I had three kids. After that statement, he called me a slut because my children didn't have the same father. It was bad. I usually didn't get to say much because he was very boisterous. He knew how to get to me and make me cry. He didn't care regardless of how much I cried. I had to leave for annual training on my job and I was so afraid to leave my kids with him because that argument occurred the morning I was scheduled to leave. At the time, I had two cars, so I called my sister and my niece. I packed my kids' clothes for school, left my niece gas money, and asked her to drop them off for school until I returned. He had no clue. I felt so much better knowing they were with my family while I was out of town. When I arrived at the hotel, I sent him a text to let him know where they were.

A few days later, I returned from training and went to the house. He was not home, so I started packing bags. A sudden fear come over me as I was packing because I didn't have anywhere to go. I didn't want to invade my mom's home and I didn't want to burden my sister. I just continued to pack. For some reason, he called me and it was small talk. At some point during that conversation, he told me I could come back to the house. I felt relief and unpacked all the clothes before he came home from work. I called my niece and she was on her way to bring my kids and drop off my car. My dad was with her and they never asked any questions. By the time he arrived, the kids were settled and I was just sitting around. He walked in, clean cut and shaved, seemingly in a better space. He was cordial and made small talk. I felt like we were mending the relationship.

It seemed like January flew by. He and I were getting along well and I was planning for the twin's birthday in February. He was putting forth an effort to help me by asking me what they wanted for their birthday and helping me brainstorm ideas for their party. A few days before their birthday, I spent the day getting some things done. I enjoyed a day of relaxation. I had lunch with a close friend of mine and we got caught up on the happenings in our lives. He was working out of town, but was calling frequently throughout the day because he was trying to pick up the twins' birthday gifts.

All I had to do was find someone to do their cake and I was done. I picked the kids up from school and started asking them about their birthday. I was surprised to learn that everything I was planning was totally opposite of what they wanted. I became irritated with them, so by the time we arrived at the house I was just over it. I told them to go in their rooms and do their homework. He called again to say he was on his way home and he had the gifts for the kids.

When he arrived home, I was sitting on the loveseat watching the news. He walked in spoke, took the kids their gifts, and came back into the living room where I was. He sat down next to me and asked if I was okay. I kept watching the news, but I answered him simply by saying I was annoyed with the kids. He sat there for a few minutes, doing some work on his laptop. I guess he became upset with me because, after a few minutes of silence, he jumped up from the loveseat, went into the

54

kitchen, and sat at the dining room table. I just looked at him. While he was sitting down he said, "You know what man, I'm just about sick of you. You probably should just leave because I'm tired of putting up with your a**."

I was still sitting on the loveseat, watching the news and without looking at him I said, "I don't care. It doesn't even matter at this point." He looked me and said, "What did you say?" I started to repeat myself but before I could get the sentence out, he jumped on me, knocked my glasses off my face, and had his hand on my face forcefully holding me down, while repeating "I'm sick of you. I'm sick of your a**." I couldn't move because he was over 200 pounds, holding me down with all his weight. When he finally let me go, I jumped up from the loveseat with tears in my eyes and looked at him. He was standing there in a fight stance with his fist up, waiting for me to attempt to hit him. I looked around and I saw the candle holder and a pair of scissors on the desk. I wanted to hit him in his temple and stab him. But the Holy Spirit prompted me to put the candle holder down, get my kids, and leave. I was crying and I began to yell for the twins to pack their clothes so we could leave. I was running through the house grabbing our things, meanwhile he ran out of the house because he figured I would call the police. He jumped in his car and sped off like a crazy person. By this time, it was pouring down raining and after grabbing as much as we could, the twins and I jumped in the car and left. I was driving around in the rain trying to figure out what I was going to do. I was crying and upset.

While I was driving, my best friend called me. When I answered the phone, she said "Hey. You were on my mind, so I am calling to check on you." I proceeded to tell her what happened and she was shocked! She said her son kept saying, "Mom call Auntie Leda and check on her." We talked as I was trying to figure out where I was going to stay. I finally called my friend who lived in the area and she told me we could come over.

As I was in route to her house, my youngest daughter's father called me to say he was dropping her off and I told him to meet me at my friend's house. I arrived at my friend's house and was a still shocked about what had happened. She was very calm, encouraged me, fixed the kids something to eat, washed and ironed their clothes, and did my oldest daughter's hair for school. As she talked to the kids to keep their minds off what they witnessed, I was on her couch looking for a hotel. I only had about $186 in the bank and I needed a room for a few nights until I figured out my next move. After calling a few places, I found us a room and when the kids' clothes were dry, I thanked my friend and we went to the hotel.

We settled in the room and the kids didn't say much. I couldn't believe I was in the hotel, basically homeless with my three kids. To make matters worse, it was a few days before the twin's birthday. After they dozed off, I couldn't sleep. I just laid there wishing I had listened to the Voice of the Lord. I blamed myself for the whole situation. I prayed as I was lying there, asking God to help me to be strong. I knew I wouldn't sleep that night, so I basically watched over my kids as they slept. While I was lying there, my phone started ringing around 2:30 a.m. It was he. I just let it ring. He called several times back-to-back. I never answered. I would not allow him to pull me back into that situation again.

The next day, I woke the kids up, prepared them for school, and dropped them off. I immediately started looking for an apartment. I was concerned because I didn't have enough established credit, which is considered bad credit. Nevertheless, I rode around until I found a townhouse I liked. I didn't apply for it right away because I wasn't sure what to do. I also knew I was down to the last few dollars in my checking account and I needed another night in the hotel. By the end of that day, my family still didn't know I was staying in the hotel. I picked my children up from school, bought dinner, and we went back to the hotel for another night. It was the last night there because I had no more money. I know my kids could sense I was worried, but they were perfect angels. They became my source of strength throughout the ordeal. Our final night at the hotel was fine, but I knew I was in a place where only God could help me. I had hit rock bottom. I knew that going back to God was my only option. I didn't know how I would come out, but I knew it had to be better than where I was.

Chapter Eight: Getting Out

We checked out of the hotel and I didn't know what to do. After I dropped the kids off at school, I drove around again looking for apartments, not certain about where to look. While I was going through everything, I had totally forgotten that I had filed my income taxes. I grabbed my phone to call and check my account. Sure enough, my income tax refund had been deposited the previous day. I was so happy and thankful because I had the means to find a place to live. I finally decided I couldn't go through the process alone, so I called my first cousin who lived in the area and I told her what happened. I told her we had stayed in a hotel for two nights and she told me to stay at her house and she would talk to her husband; but she was certain it would be fine with him. I started to feel some sense of relief. She had an extra bedroom that the kids and I could stay in until I got on my feet. I was in between jobs and I didn't start my new job until March 4.

I went to her house after talking with her and she greeted me with a hug. We sat down and I told her what happened; she was furious! She was glad I had gotten out of there. I told her I was looking for an apartment and she advised me where I should look. I told her about the town house that was for rent and she suggested I apply for get it. I went to apply for the townhouse and the waiting seemed like it took forever. In the meantime, I stayed with my cousin and went through all the emotions that I was feeling because of the break-up. I was cooking, cleaning, doing whatever I could to not cry.

I still hadn't told my parents and siblings about my situation but I knew I would have to eventually. I was in the process of getting braces and I had to have a few of my teeth extracted prior to getting them. I went to get them extracted and afterwards, I went to see my mom. I told her what happened, where we were staying, and that I'd already applied for an apartment. I was just waiting to hear back. She encouraged me to call while I was there with her. I called to check on the status of my application and the manager informed that it was still being processed. I was praying for some good news soon!

Although I was staying with my cousin, I still needed to go back to the house and pack our clothing. I was there one day and my phone rang as I was about to wash a load of clothes. It was the manager of the apartment complex informing me that I met the qualifications for the townhouse and she wanted to know if I was available to meet at 3:00 p.m. to view the space. I excitedly agreed and I grabbed my keys to leave. I put the dirty clothes in my car and I went to start the car and it was dead. I tried it again and nothing happened. I had both of my cars in the garage, but one was blocking the other. I was desperate; it was already a quarter to three and I needed to figure something out quick! I stood in the garage looking at both cars trying to figure out a solution. So, I did what any other desperate mother would do: I put my Galant in neutral and pushed it, while turning the wheel to straighten it out so that I could get my Altima out of the garage. Amazingly, it took me about five minutes to do that and I only had another five minutes to meet the manager to view the apartment. As I was driving a across town, my cousin called to check on me. I told her that I was on my way to look at the apartment and she agreed to meet me there. Once I arrived at the manager's office, I trailed her to view the property. A few minutes later, my cousin arrived and we looked at the apartment.

I was very pleased because it was spacious: had three bedrooms, two-and-a-half bathrooms, and a private patio. I agreed to take the apartment and we went back to her office where I happily gave her a deposit. I was beyond excited!

After I paid my deposit, I went back to my cousin's house and we sat around talking about the whole situation that occurred. As we were talking, my phone rang. It was he.

Me: "Hello".

Him: "Hey. How you doing?"

Me: "I'm fine."

Him: "I tried to catch you while you were at the house the other day because I wanted us to talk. I figured we could sit down and talk to the kids and go to church on Sunday.

Me: (thinking to myself: we haven't been going to church), "No, because I've already found a place and I'm getting ready to move. The kids and I were in a hotel for two nights."

Him: (Immediately becomes angry) "That's your d*** fault, didn't nobody tell you to leave! Alright, you need to have your s*** out by Saturday at 5:00!"

I hung up and immediately started crying! My cousin was sitting in the living room and she told me to stop crying. She picked up her phone and called her employer. She looked at me and said, "Don't worry about it, I just took the day off; we'll go get your things and get storage until you can move in your apartment." I got on the phone called my mom, dad, and siblings. I told them what he said and they told me not to worry. My oldest sister asked for his phone number. She called him to let him know we were going to the house to pack my things and move me out. He was cordial with her and agreed. She wanted to make sure there would not be any problems. Of course, he said to her, "No, it's not a problem!"

As my cousin and I waited for the rest of the family, she called around to see if she could find a truck. Thankfully, her husband borrowed a truck from a friend. As my family started to

61

show up at my cousin's house, it was all surreal to me. I didn't say it to them, but I was so embarrassed by the whole situation. I could not believe it was my life, but at the same time I was grateful for the love and support of my family. Once everyone arrived, we all went over to the house to pack my things. When I walked through the door, it was eerie. I was just in a hurry to get my things and get out! It was obvious he hadn't done any cleaning since I left. The bed was unmade; there were dishes in the sink and dirty clothes (his) in the floor. It was a mess, by my standards anyway. I told everyone where our things were, gave them suitcases, and they went to it. Along with my mom, sister, and cousin, I started packing my things. As I went to the closet to grab my clothes, I noticed that he had put my valentine's gift on my side of the closet. I didn't want it, so I left it there. I wanted nothing but to get out!

A few hours into the packing and some cleaning (we did him a favor), we finally got everything out of the house. There was a storage house in the back yard with my furniture and as we were taking it out, we realized it was ruined. Apparently, there was a hole in the roof (which he knew about) and the kids' beds, mattresses, and my other personal items were all ruined. I could not use them. I was going to need new beds and furniture. I was so upset, but I couldn't do anything about it. We loaded up everything for the day and took it to the storage facility. The only items left to move were my washer, dryer, and a few other large items.

The next day my dad, cousin and cousin's husband arrived to help move the washer and dryer. We could move that quickly and get it to storage. I could sell most of the items that were ruined because of the rain to a lady at a local thrift store. Because they were not in the best shape, I told her $50.00 was fine, since she insisted on giving me something. I was finally out of the house of horror. My things were in storage and I had a few days until I signed my lease and moved into my apartment. Over the next few days, I tried to keep myself occupied as much as possible! I kept going to the storage. I was cleaning my cousin's house and they came home one day to find me cooking not one, but two lasagnas! I was just trying to cope with my circumstances and the anger that I felt. I honestly knew that I would be in jail for killing my ex, if I could get away with it. He was so mean to me. The anger I felt was a direct result of how he had treated me. When I wasn't cooking or cleaning, I was listening to slow jams on my phone. It was a recipe for disaster!

The day finally arrived for me to sign my lease and move into my apartment. I was excited to be in my own space, and to try to deal with all my feelings on my own. I signed my lease, got my keys, and slowly got everything moved in a week before orientation on my new job. I was happy when I was around other people; but when I was alone, I struggled with my feelings and emotions. It was hard. I've always considered myself a resilient type of person, but I didn't know how I was going to bounce back from the type of hurt I was feeling. I had never felt so much anger toward anyone in my life. I was hurting not only for myself, but for my children as well. It was a tough place to be in emotionally. I tried to cope with it by going out, partying, and drinking, but that would only dull the pain for a while. I remember thinking, "How in the hell did I get back here?" I had been delivered from that type of life, but I found myself back there and I didn't know how or if I could come out of such a place of darkness.

As time went on, I became more and more depressed. I tried to mask it during the day, but at night in my home with my children, I was horrible. I had become him! I would curse my kids, I was very withdrawn, and did not engage my kids at all. I was more focused on what I was going through and not considering that my children were just as affected as I was by the whole situation. I finally decided that no one could help me out of the hell and darkness I was in, but God. I had to go back to

God; surrender and give it all to him. To do that, I had to pray, meditate, and repent. I had to truly give God total control of my life. One night, as I was going through my typical sort of depressed mood, the Lord told me to write. I knew at that moment I had to get my feelings out through words. So, I started journaling. Here is my first entry:

February 25, 2013

"And Jesus said unto them, I am the bread of life: he that cometh to me shall never hunger, and he that believeth on me shall never thirst" (John 6: 35).

I have been through quite a transition in the past week. I decided that maybe I should write about my feelings instead of keeping them bottled up. I thought it would be appropriate to have a scripture and John 6: 35 seem fitting for my situation right now. In this verse, the Lord is saying if we surrender unto him, we shall not want anything. There is eternal life in God. Why depend on "man" when God's promises do not return void. This is so relevant to me right now! I put my hope in and gave my love to a man whom I thought was my soulmate. Unfortunately, it turned out that he was not the man I thought he was. I didn't expect him to do what he did and it was disappointing. I know God knew and He allowed the situation to occur to help me get back to where I needed to be. I can't deny the fact that I still love him, but at this point I must pray, shift my focus, and do what is pleasing to God. I am so blessed to still be on this earth and I am so grateful that God did not give up on me. I have a purpose and I am going to do what is right! Sometimes, I must encourage myself. I will stand in 2013!

That first entry empowered me and gave me hope for the future of my family. I felt like we were going to be alright. I felt like I could get back to a place of peace and reconnect with the Lord.

It was not easy trying to get back to that place where I had been before I met him. I had been in a place of peace and contentment with the life I had with my children. I never stressed marriage or a long-term relationship because I was so focused on my relationship with God, family, and career. But I have learned the devil does not like anything that is going in the direction of God's Will. Nevertheless, I was determined to overcome everything I'd been through. I was excited to write at the end of every day because it was like a release for me. I was shedding all the verbal abuse, emotional abuse, and physical abuse I endured during the relationship. Here is my second journal entry.

February 26, 2013

"Pray without ceasing" (I Thessalonians 5:17).

This verse is important to me because if it had not been for someone constantly praying for me, I don't know where I would be! I feel like those prayers and God's grace are what have kept me. I'm so grateful because I, too, have learned to pray all the time, as prayer is essential for a connection with God. I'm at a point in my life where I feel like I must reconnect with God, so I am thankful for the opportunity to pray. I thank God for not giving up on me. We must pray every day! It is prayer that keeps us. If we are sinners, God still hears us. He desires us to pray because He is not pleased with sin. He does not shun us, but He hears us. How great is that! We can't take God's grace for granted. I will continue to pray to get me through my 'now'. I'm ready for the next level!

I thought journaling would make me feel better about my life and what I had recently experienced. My date for starting my new job was approaching fast and I wasn't ready mentally or emotionally. I knew no matter how much I talked about it with my mom, my best friend, or other friends; it still wouldn't change what I was struggling with internally. I felt so embarrassed because after the relationship ended so many people came to me and said "You didn't know he was crazy?" or "I didn't know he was in a relationship, let alone engaged!" and my favorite, "He always dates women not from here because everyone knows how he is in our hometown." I wanted to go somewhere and hide most days. I stayed up most nights crying and thinking about everything that had happened in my life. I found myself journaling about it too.

February 28, 2013

"Come unto me, all ye that labour and are heavy laden, and I will give you rest" (Matthew 11:28).

Wow! I just read my devotional for today. It is so relevant to what I feel right now! For the longest time, I have carried a sense of guilt for the sudden change in my lifestyle nine months ago when I moved in with a man who was not my husband and I thought I would be alright. However, I realized because of who I am and the call the Lord has on my life, I could not rest. I prayed every night asking and seeking God's forgiveness. I had prayer, praise, and worship in my car every morning on my way to work because I desperately needed to hear from God. Even though I knew I wasn't supposed to be in the house with that man, I stayed. Because of that decision, I became more and more concerned about what God thought of me than what I thought of that man. I started having panic attacks and had nights where I could not lay in bed beside him. I knew God had already brought me through so much and I honestly thought God would NOT forgive me. But what I have learned is that God knows all: the beginning, the middle, and the end. He knew how the situation would end. After over a year of being in a relationship with this man and nine months of living with him, God has brought me out. He has removed me from that sinful situation. Now, even though I'm out of the situation, I still can't rest. I know that is the enemy who seeks to torture me. I know that that man is not of God's will. God knows I desire a man after His own heart, who will seek Him to find me. What I desire is for God to restore me, restore my soul and draw me closer unto Him. I know God will do this for me because His grace is sufficient.

So, first God says, come to me with all your guilt, sins and weariness and He will give us rest. He will forgive us. Then He says to those of us who are broken, He will heal and/or mend our broken spirits. God is amazing! Our God is truly an awesome God. Only He can give us His grace and then forgive us. I am so grateful for His grace. I'm grateful that God knows my broken spirit and my desire to do His Will.

I was so afraid God would give up on me while I was in my mess. He gave me signs; told me when to leave, and I didn't. As things sometimes happen, God had to get my attention so that I could be obedient. He allowed my ex to show his true self. I was on a path to reconnect with God. I know that reconnecting with God meant that I had to totally trust Him, repent, surrender all, not give in to the depressed moods I felt, forgive my ex, step out on faith, and release fear. But more than anything, I had to pray. I needed to hear God. I knew it would be a long journey, but I was not willing to give up. I was determined to get back to me!

Chapter Nine: Trusting God

The kids and I were settled in our new place and trying to get back to a sense of normalcy. They were seemingly alright, but it was one-day-at-a-time for me. I wanted so desperately not to feel the anger and hurt I felt daily. I was getting closer to starting my new job and I knew that I would just have to 'grin and bear it'. I spent most of my nights crying, lying in my bed, and thinking about how I had lost myself in that relationship. I was trying to figure out how to get back to 'me'. Regardless of what I felt, writing in my journal was a way to express myself. In this chapter, I will share my journal entries that were written during that time of my life. I was in a dark place and God sometimes used others to help me see that. There were moments when I felt strong, but most of the time I felt beaten down by life and what I endured. It was truly a struggle--one from which I knew only God could deliver me.

March 2, 2013

"I can do all things through Christ which strengthens me" (Philippians 4:13).

Whoa! This is an awesome scripture because it is my favorite scripture! I have recently gone through an unexpected, but somewhat expected transition. It was sudden, but God graced me with His favor to recover! When men think that they have knocked you on your face, God always has a ram in the bush. It is by His might that I could get what I needed in a timely manner. One thing about God, He is always on time! I mean when He does something, it's a quick turnaround! It is because of my faith in Him that I have the strength I need to move forward. When I woke up on Friday, God gave me a scripture. It was "Study to show thyself approved unto God, a workman that needed not to be ashamed, rightly dividing the word of truth" (2 Timothy 2:15).

I thought "Okay God!" I must get myself together and go forth with what God has told me. I am going to read, study, and prepare myself for a new level. It is scary, but God gives us no more than we can handle. I am so excited about the new direction in which my life is going. It seems like things are already looking better. Praise God!

After each entry, I felt a little better. I knew that I had a long way to go, but I was not willing to give up and let the enemy win. There were some days, I felt good emotionally and then there were days that I just wanted to stay in bed and cry all day. I was in a dark place. In the meantime, I still had to be mom to my children. I still struggled with interacting with them daily because I couldn't get beyond what I was feeling. It was tough. Nevertheless, I started my new job and prepared for my new beginning.

March 4, 2013

"But seek ye first the kingdom of God, and his righteousness, and these things shall be added unto you" (Matthew 6:33).

Today I started a new job. I am so grateful to God for this opportunity to make a fresh start. The scripture tells us to seek God first and He will add unto us accordingly. How simple is that? I feel like I am finally in a better place where I am determined to stay in God's will. I have truly experienced what I call "supernatural favor" from God. He opened doors for me and helped me get to a better place. I will say God had to allow me to get to my lowest point because I was homeless and living in a hotel. I didn't know where I would lay my head or where my children would lay their heads. But, I thank God for my family and how they came together to help me. I will continue to seek His will and let God put everything into place. Thy will be done and not my own! In Jesus name! Amen! Praise God!

So, my first day at work was not so bad. I was not as friendly, but I wasn't so withdrawn either. I made it through and I was looking forward to better days.

March 5, 2013

"Confess your faults one to another and pray one for another that ye may be healed. The effectual fervent prayer of a righteous man availeth much" (James 5:16).

Sometimes I wonder if God hears my prayers. I felt like He didn't hear me anymore because he was tired of me. I thought I was not worthy for Him to hear and/or answer my prayers. However, what I have learned over the years is that when I call on the Name of Jesus the devil must flee! There is a shift in the atmosphere just by saying J-E-S-U-S! I understand that God wants me/us to pray not only when times in our lives are good, but it is during those trying times that the Lord really wants us to come to Him. I have been guilty of finding it difficult to go to God during trying times because I was focusing on the situation, wallowing in self-pity, and trying to resolve the issues myself. If we just confess our faults, the scripture says we can be healed. That is powerful! God loves us even when we think He has given up on us.

Over the years, I've had some special experiences with God. I've always known I was different, but I just didn't know how or what to do. Even when things were going well, I still felt a sense of sadness. Recently, a good friend of mine told me "Leda, you always have sadness about you. I think you try to find things/people to make you happy, but it doesn't work out. I think you need to accept whatever it is God wants you to do and then you will be happy." I was literally dumb founded. I said, "Really?" She responded. "Yes!" I felt like that was profound insight with a message for me. So even amid the emotional pain, hurt, and turmoil that I feel, I continue to move forward. I know that with God, I will be alright. I'm thankful that even when I was lost in my sin and felt like I couldn't get out, God still heard my prayers. I'm so grateful because I'm here. I lived to fight another day. For that, Lord, I truly say, "Thank you!"

I will never forget those words my friend spoke to me that day. I knew she was right and the Lord used her to remind me that I had to accept the calling He has on my life. Just hearing it from her solidified it for me.

March 6, 2013

"Thy kingdom come. Thy will be done in earth, as it is in heaven" (Matthew 6:10).

So, this scripture is much needed for me this week! I have struggled with my feelings all week! Whew! It is sometimes hard to stop loving a person when your heart doesn't want to. I keep reminding myself that God has something greater for me. I keep saying it is God's will, not my will. Ultimately what we should focus on is God's will and forget about our will. We should agree with God's will for our lives no matter how much we struggle to accept it. I think a part of God's will for us is also our purpose. God has a purpose for our lives and even if he has to snatch us out of our situation to get us there, he will. What I'm learning is God has a plan and I have to accept it. I should accept what God allows to happen in my life. Ultimately, I am grateful to God for removing me from that situation. God knew all along, but He had to get my attention or I would still be there. I'm looking forward to walking in my destiny and staying in GOD'S WILL! This is my desire and my prayer.

March 7, 2013

"He healeth the broken in heart, and bindeth up their wounds" (Psalm 147:3).

I think I needed to find this verse. It just confirms what I've been praying. Right now, I feel like my heart is in pieces. I feel like I'm slowly beginning to mend. I know I can't do it, but God will. I pray for each day to get better. I pray that God will empower me to be the great person He has called me to be. I want to be pleasing to God. My heart hurts, but I trust God for healing my heart. I trust God that I will be a witness and help other women who may have gone through a domestic situation. I praise God daily because I'm still alive. Every day is another chance for me to get my life together. "God, I accept what You have allowed in my life. I accept Your plan for my life. I seek Your forgiveness and ask that You make me over and let Your light shine through me. God, I want to be a witness to others. I want to walk in my purpose. Thank you, Lord! I know the best is yet to come!"

March 8, 2013

"We love him because he first loved us" (I John 4:19).

The past three weeks have been weeks of transition for me and my children. I am blessed beyond measure because God continues to show me favor despite my sins. I was reminded of the song, 'Jesus loves me'. If I don't know anything else, I know Jesus loves ME! He loves me even when I don't love myself. The scripture says because He first loved us, we love Him. I'm so grateful for God's love and His grace. I feel He is truly healing my heart and preparing me for my purpose. I have always desired to be pleasing in His eyes. I don't want to leave this world and not be helpful to someone. I desire to make a difference. That is truly my heart's desire. I'm going to work on those dreams the Lord gave me years ago. I can't keep sleeping on God's promises for me. I am so ready for God's will to be done in my life and the lives of my children.

At this point in the book, I've shared with you some of my journal entries that were written after the relationship. I will continue to do that; however, these next entries are not in order as the previous ones were.

March 12, 2013

I Corinthians 6:20

"For ye are brought with a price: therefore, glorify God in your body and in your spirit, which are God's."

Well, today I thank God for life and just waking up and seeing another day. For the first time in a month, I feel good. I'm encouraged by what God is doing in my life. I'm so thankful for the doors He opened for me. It is truly my desire to be a vessel for the Lord and to share His goodness. I love today's scripture because after all that I've endured, I forgot that I belong to God! I am His child. I love the Lord! He does not give me the spirit of fear; He gives me peace, love and a sound mind! I will conquer my spirit of fear! The devil wants me to give in to it, but I refuse to do so! I declare I am healed, I am whole and I am victorious. No one can love us like the Lord. I am so thankful that I know my destiny is in His hands. By God's stripes I am healed and set free! By His stripes, I (we) are redeemed. What more can we ask for?!

March 13, 2013

"What then shall we say to these things? If God is for us, who is against us" (Romans 8:31).

I am so thankful for brighter days! I'm still fighting and I'm determined to win. This battle is not mine; it is truly the Lord's. I don't know what God has in store for me, but I'm not afraid to go forward. I thank God for healing my brokenness and He is going to build me back up to be even greater. My sister told me the Lord said, "What's to come is what's greater than what has been." I truly believe that. I know that God has something in store for me. I don't know about dating, marriage, or relationships, but I know God first, family, and everything else after that. I'm going to keep seeking the Lord's will for me life. At this point, I can't afford to waste any more time. I'm happy and I like what I see when I look in the mirror. I feel like God is FINALLY pleased with me and that makes me happy. I still have some issues I'm working out, but God is able! I am better because of my circumstance.

March 14, 2013

"And let us not be weary in well doing: for in due season we shall reap if we faint not" (Galatians 6:9).

I was thinking this evening about what my mom told me on Christmas Day last year when I was going through a difficult time. My mom quoted that verse and encouraged me to keep doing good. She said, "I know it hurts, but it will work out." I couldn't understand why a person (my ex) could be so cold-hearted and purposely mean. On December 25, 2102, my heart was broken. I think I knew already because God had given me an answer and a plan. I told my mom I was leaving and I knew I had to go. I was so tired and I just felt like I couldn't make it. I never knew what it was to love a man so much, or so I thought. But, I started to lean on God and let Him take care of me. So, now I am free and no longer do I feel weary in my well doing. I'm so happy because God is pleased with me. I know He is my keeper, supplier of my needs and my way maker. Even though I have moments where I feel angry and I feel pure hate, I know it is not pleasing to God. So, instead I will pray for that man who caused me so much pain. I pray that he will draw unto God for help and that he will become a better father, brother, son, uncle and friend. I pray for God to heal the hurt, anger, and disappointment in his heart. I pray God's protection over him and I sincerely pray that he doesn't abuse another woman. Although God is healing me, I wish for no other woman to experience abuse at his hands. I just want to be free and put all thoughts of him and the abuse behind me. I am healed! I am set free because God is my redeemer!

March 23, 2013

"Casting the whole of your care [all anxieties, all worries, all concerns, once and for all] on Him, for He cares for you affectionately and cares about you watchfully" (I Peter 5:7, AMP Bible).

I love this verse! This is an awesome verse because the Lord says to cast ALL (that means everything!) our cares upon Him. God does not want us to worry or suffer with stress. It is so great to know He loves us so much that He's willing to take on all of our concerns. There is no man or woman on this earth who's willing to do that. How great is our God? As a single mother, I often worry about money and bills; today I was surely worried. But, I rest in God that He is a way maker! I know God is an on-time God and He has not failed me. It is to Him we should look, trust, and, depend upon. In the past month-and-a-half, I've realized that God IS MY HELP!

I know all these things that happened to me are not in vain. When I was literally homeless and didn't know if I could or would find a place, it was God to whom I turned. It was God who was my comforter. He relieved my worries and made a way out of no way. Even when I couldn't see past what was in front of me, God knew it would all work out for my good. I will continue to cast my cares upon the Lord. I'm blessed to be alive and I'm thankful for God's continuous grace and mercy. I'm grateful for His love, favor, and the strength He continues to give me. I truly praise God for my life.

March 28, 2013

"When thou liest down, thou shalt not be afraid; yea, thou shalt lie down, and thy sleep shall be sweet" (Proverbs 3:24).

The verse is simple: God promises us sweet sleep! We should not be afraid when we lay down to rest. I can recall for months how I struggled, trying to sleep and I always looked as if I was going through a struggle; but God! I'm so grateful that today I walk in the spirit of God. We have to remember that God gives us blessings and does not bring confusion. He brings us peace, joy, laughter, and He teaches us humility.

I am humbled that God is faithful to be just and fair. I will continue to seek God to heal my heart and to help me forgive those who have hurt me. I'm in expectation of something. My heart is overwhelmed with joy as I seem to become stronger with each passing day. It is my desire to have a husband who loves the Lord, who can respect me as a celibate woman, and help me get to my level in God. I don't know what's to come, but it surely will be better than what has been! I praise God in advance for new beginnings!

April 7, 2013

"Be careful for nothing, but everything by prayer and supplication with thanksgiving let your requests be made known unto God (Philippians 4:6).

I finally found this scripture! I see what God is saying to me! I'm so grateful to our heavenly father for the gift of words/writing. I don't know where this will lead me, but I truly desire to share my story with the world. Lord, I want to start to work on my dream. I feel it is time! I have been delayed and denied long enough. I know I've made some bad twists and turns, but now, God, I'm ready to walk the path that you have destined for me. The scripture says "Be anxious for nothing...but by prayer and supplication... make your requests known unto God."

I know it was the Lord who placed this scripture in my spirit! We can't afford to be anxious because often being anxious leads us to do things that are not of God. If we petition God for our desires, He is sure to fulfill them. God is NOT like man; He will not lie. We have to consider that God is a gracious God. He keeps giving us "do overs" because every new day is a chance to get our lives right. I know I have a testimony because God has given me many, many chances and I'm so grateful! I thank God for His strength He has given me to walk away from a sinful situation. It was not where I wanted to be; but God! I'm thankful God renewed my spirit and He continues to touch my heart.

I am going to walk in my purpose. I want to please God, not man. I'm so excited about what's to come. I speak life, victory, peace, financial blessings, and breakthroughs over my life, the lives of my children and my family. My dreams will come to pass! I believe God's promises for me and they will not return void. I know God has a plan and I pray His will be done in my life!

April 11, 2013

"For I know the thoughts that I think toward you, saith Jehovah, thoughts of peace and not evil to give you hope in your latter end. And ye shall call upon me and I will hearken unto you. And ye shall seek me, and find me, when ye shall search for me with all your heart" (Jeremiah 29: 11-13).

To paraphrase: God is saying hold on, hold out, don't give up. Don't give in to discouragement; success is up ahead, not suffering. You will turn back to Him and ask for help and He will answer your prayers. God continues by saying you will worship Him with all your heart and He will be with you and accept your worship.

I thank God for leading me to those scriptures. Sometimes I feel as if I'm walking in a daze. I wonder if I am meeting my purpose in life. I feel like I am just here! I know only God can fill that void that is on the inside me. I reflect over my life and I feel like I've wasted so much time. I don't want to do anything else displeasing to God. I don't want to sit on my dreams anymore! I'm trying and God knows, hears, and sees all. I'm so blessed to be among the living. God has kept me, even amid my sin! I desire to lead a life pleasing to God; helping others and encouraging young girls/women who have been through similar situations. I don't want to feel like I am not doing things within my purpose.

God gives us this precious life. We have a choice; we can live for Him or choose not to live for Him. Its life or death; no lukewarm or in between! I know I've been guilty of living in fear and that is surely not of God. The scripture says, "The Lord does not give us the spirit of fear, but of peace and love, and a sound mind." That is powerful because there are people in this world who want to have those things, but don't know how to get them. I thank God for peace and a sound mind. I'm not perfect, but I thank God for His grace and mercy. I'm redeemed from sin and I am free! Praise God!

April 14, 2013

"Now faith is the substance of things hoped for the evidence of things not seen" (Hebrews 11:1).

"But without faith it is impossible to please him: for he that cometh to God must believe that he is, and that he is a rewarder of them that diligently seek him" (Hebrews 11:6).

The Lord says 'now faith,' your 'right now faith' is the foundation that we need. God is our rewarder if we seek Him daily. If we read Hebrews 11, we find that the Lord is talking to us about faith. He speaks of Noah who was warned of things that were not yet seen. He also speaks about Abraham who went out to a foreign place not knowing where he was. Because of his obedience and his faith, he was rewarded openly. The scripture speaks of Sarah, whose faith was so strong that she believed she could conceive; even when she was past the age of childbearing. Faith is the substance of things hoped for and the evidence of things unseen. We must have that 'NOW FAITH'! We can't have faith when things are going well for us and then doubt when there is a struggle. The scripture says He is a rewarder of those who diligently seek Him. It is imperative that we spend time with God daily; our faith /hope should not lie in man. Our faith is always in God. God is not like man and I think we often forget that because God does not move in our time. All things are in God's time. We must remember that His time is always ON TIME! I can recall when I was struggling on my last job because I was so weary. I thought God had forgotten about me. My mom kept telling me to just trust God. I felt like I had little faith in the fact that I would ever leave that job. I decided to stop dwelling on it and focus on doing my absolute best while I was on that job. I must admit, some days were harder than others, but

I saw my way through. One Friday after months of waiting, I received a call about a job. The human resources representative said, "I have a position for you that meets your background and past experiences." I was floored, but even more in awe of the favor God had placed on me. It had been over three months since my initial interview with the human resource coordinator; But God!

Since that time, God has opened some doors for me (and closed some) in a way I couldn't possibly explain. It was a quick turnaround. My faith in God is totally restored and I will continue to seek Him daily. He is slowly restoring me. He is my keeper and my help. I trust God and my faith is strong even when I can't see a way. God continues to show up and show out for me and my family. That is what I describe as 'NOW FATIH'! I trust that even when I can't see beyond my circumstances, that God's Will be done in my life.

April 22, 2013

"But godliness with contentment is great gain" (I Timothy 6:6).

"Let your conversation be without covetousness; and be content with such things as ye have: for he hath said, I will never leave thee, nor forsake thee" (Hebrews 13:5).

As I do daily, I thank the Lord for life; the lives of my children, and my family. I desire so much from the Lord, right now. I feel like the best is yet to come. In such a day and time as this, we must be prayerful and rely on God's Word/promises for us. We must not forget that His Word does not return void. I'm studying and focusing on contentment because that is an area with which I'm struggling. I must learn to be content with what the Lord has given me. If I have God and contentment, then according to the word, that will be great gain. He further tells us in Hebrews to not covet in conversation, but again be content because He will not leave us or forsake us! This is so awesome! I know that God will always be there for me. It is not good for us to worry because God is the supplier of all our needs. God reminded me that we must not be weary in well doing. Instead, we should focus on praising God in advance for the blessings to come. We are truly blessed beyond measure!

April 30, 2013

"Create in me a clean heart, O God; and renew a right spirit within me" (Psalms 51:10).

Today, as I do every day, I thank God, our heavenly father for our lives. Thank you for the constant reminder that you give me daily in my spirit and bring me back to You! No matter what, I knew in my heart I always had to go back to God. I'm most grateful that God accepted me!

The scripture above is my mom's favorite verse in the bible. She says that verse is powerful because God can renew/refresh us with His spirit. He can create in us a clean heart, if we ask. I read a status on social media that said, "Hold God accountable." God cannot, shall not, and will not lie. What God said will come to pass. He further says "If you dive in faith, He promises not to let you drown. For your blessing is in the water." How powerful is that? We can trust that God's Word does not return void! If He can create in "me" (us) a clean heart, then He will certainly fulfill His promises to us. I'm grateful because despite everything, I truly know Jesus is love.

Those are some of my journal entries that were significant to me during my time of depression. I was in such a dark place; I didn't know if I would come out. If it were not for the Lord giving me the words to write and leading me to scriptures, I would not be free today. I was so bound by hurt and anger, that even others could see it. No matter how much I tried to hide it, I couldn't do so. I even had a co-worker to tell me how I seemed dark physically and spiritually. I was embarrassed, but I knew if he noticed it, he was in tune with the Holy Spirit. I could no longer let the devil defeat me. I spent many nights crying, praying, and asking God to heal my heart. He truly became my comfort when I felt like I couldn't get through that season in my life. I realized I had to pick myself up because my children started to notice and express to me how I made them feel because of my actions. I had to stop being selfish and start being a mom again.

I sat my kids down and we talked it out. I told them to forgive my ex because holding on to unforgiveness was not pleasing to God. What I learned during that conversation was how angry my son was. I learned that while we were living with my ex, at some point he had choked my son until he almost passed out. My oldest daughter witnessed it and that created so much hate toward him by my son. I learned that my son was very afraid of this man. Although he didn't tell me about my ex choking him until we were out of the house, I felt guilty. I had no clue. At that moment, I had to pray for my crying son. He said he felt helpless because he watched my ex put his hands on me and he didn't do anything. I told my son that not doing something was the best thing he could have done. Had he attempted to do something, someone may have gotten seriously hurt. As he cried, I prayed for him. I had to be the example for my children. I had to tell my son that hitting a woman is never the right thing to do. He was so full of anger and he admitted that he wanted "to kill" my ex for what he did to me. That was a light bulb moment for me because I saw his hurt and anger. It became very apparent to me at that moment.

It was from that moment on that I prayed for my children every night. I told my son to forgive and encouraged him daily. I didn't want him to feel defeated because he didn't protect me. The whole domestic situation took a toll on my kids more than I had imagined. It was because of them that I found the strength to fight my way from darkness. I could no longer afford to go home, hide in my room, and not interact with my kids. I was being selfish and not facing the problem at hand. I kept praying for deliverance. I kept seeking God's Will even when I struggled. I cried like never before, but those tears were cleansing for me. I finally began to realize that I am not my past. I wanted to see beyond my circumstances because it was taking so much energy to walk around in defeat. But, most of all I had to show my kids that I was not defeated. I was their only example of how to show love. I refused to show them anything less. It was God Who helped me to get to a place of forgiveness. I'm grateful because were it not for Him, I don't know if I would be the person I am today.

Chapter Ten: The Shift

After more than a year of struggling to overcome depression and anger, I finally started to feel good about myself. That year was probably one of the most difficult times of my life. I was struggling to overcome my own emotional issues, but I still had to go work and provide therapy for my clients. I learned so much about myself during that time. I felt like I was truly a strong person because amid my hurt, I made it my business to help my clients. I started off my new job kind of rocky because I was still in that dark place, but I'm thankful for my supervisor. She saw that I was struggling one day and she called me into her office. It was not a pleasant exchange, but instead of writing me up, she asked me if she could pray for me. She saw my potential, but my effort was minimal. She knew I was capable of doing much better than I was presenting at the time. She prayed for me (I was ugly crying the whole time) and it was like I felt an instant release. She hugged me (as I continued to cry) and reassured me everything would be alright. From that moment on, I was better. I appreciate my supervisor for that. I'd never had one like her before; she was truly set apart from the rest.

As time went on, my prayers and my journal entries shifted. I started writing about strength, healing, faith, understanding, asking, restoration, obedience, husband (s), patience, and encouragement. I had no idea why the Lord had me to focus on those areas. Regardless, I had to be obedient and continue to let the spirit lead me. I can recall during that time in my life how weak I felt. It was so difficult for me. It was a struggle to get out of bed and go to work most days. I remember calling on the Lord for strength. It wasn't just the fact that I felt weak physically, but I also felt weak spiritually and mentally. My will to fight was gone. It's not surprising that the first scriptures the Lord led me to focused on was strength. Here are a few that I constantly prayed during that time.

" The Lord is my strength and song, and is become my salvation. (Psalms 118:14).

"God is our refuge and strength, a very present help in trouble" (Psalms 46:1).

" Seek the Lord and his strength, seek his face continually" (I Chronicles 16:11).

"In God is my salvation and my glory: the rock of my strength and my refuge is in God" (Psalms 62:7).

"Strength and honour are her clothing; and she shall rejoice in time to come" (Psalms 31:25).

I leaned on God's Word and His promises for my strength and my joy. I couldn't see it at the time, but God was a constant help for me. What was so prevalent during that time was the fact that all my so-called friends were gone. I had no one. At the time, I felt some type of way about them, but now I realize I needed that time for me and God. My friends couldn't help me through that situation; I had to go to God on my own. So, I found my strength, my help, and my will in the Lord. I spent many nights crying, praying, and calling out to God because I was tired of feeling weak! He became my rock, my refuge, and my ultimate strength.

Once I felt I had my strength back, I still needed more. I was still broken and I wanted to be whole. I needed to be healed. I don't mean physically, but I needed healing from my sin. I needed to be healed from my hurt. I needed God to restore me. These are the scriptures that I was led to:

"Have mercy upon me Lord; for I am weak: O Lord heal me, for my bones are vexed" (Psalms 6:2).

"Heal me, O Lord, and I shall be healed; save me, and I shall be saved: for thou art my praise" (Jeremiah 17:14).

"Lord be merciful unto me: heal my soul; for I have sinned against thee" (Psalms 41:4).

"Return, ye backsliding children, and I will heal your backslidings. Behold, we come unto thee: for thou art the Lord our God" (Jeremiah 3: 22).

I took the Word and I meditated on it. I needed that Word more than I needed anything else. No man on earth could help me with the healing I needed. I was literally walking around like I was going to explode. At this point, I was over the relationship, but I was caught up in being a victim. When I had that victim mindset, it was even more difficult for me to get the breakthrough that I needed from God. So, the Lord said, "I will heal you. I will restore you. I will make you new again." He did just that. When He did it, I was truly a new person. I couldn't necessarily explain it, but I could see it and feel it. I was free. I felt totally free from the reminder of my sins, my relationships, and all those negative things, of which, the enemy tried to constantly remind me.

At this point, God was totally doing a new thing in me. He gave me my strength and will back; He healed and restored me. Then the Lord led me to study faith. I was at a point where my faith was minimal. I wasn't sure about much of anything because of the cycle of disappointments that occurred in my life. Nevertheless, I was obedient and began to study faith.

"For we walk by faith, not by sight" (II Corinthians 5:7).

"And he said unto them, Why are ye so fearful? how is it that ye have no faith" (Mark 4:40).

"For therein is the righteousness of God revealed from faith to faith: as it is written, The just shall live by faith" (Romans 1: 17).

"Yea, a man may say, Thou has faith, and I have works: shew me thy faith without thy works, and I will shew thee my faith by my works" (James 2:18).

"And Jesus answering saith unto them, Have faith in God" (Mark 11: 22).

I struggled because I had put more faith in man than the Lord. Let me say that again. I had more faith in man, than I did the Lord. That was my problem. How could I do that? I started seeing man doing more for me (which is what the enemy wanted me to believe) than God. When the devil set me up, he created a façade and I was blinded. Once I began to pray, trust the Lord, and put my faith in Him, my mindset was different. When I was faced with a situation, I didn't worry because I had faith that the Lord would work it out. To date, He hasn't failed me, and my faith is restored. I've learned that God's timing is not our timing and no matter what the situation, have faith and trust the Lord to work it out. Strength, healing, and faith are just a few of God's promises for us. God will strengthen you when you feel weak, and He will heal you physically, mentally, emotionally, and spiritually. Finally, have faith in God--not man-- that He will supply your needs. If He did it for me, I know without a doubt He can do it for you.

As I continued to write and pray, the Lord continued to lead me to more scriptures. I started to write on understanding, asking, and restoring.

I wrote this at a time when I was dealing with my own issues. I think before I could get past the hurt and the initial disappointment, I wanted an understanding. But no matter how I tried to rationalize it, I couldn't make sense of anything that was going on in my life at the time. It was like I was living my life on repeat. I was so over being hurt by people and I didn't understand how or why I could allow certain things to happen. I've come to terms with the fact that mistakes happen in life, but I had to learn from them. I didn't plan on being involved in certain situations that occurred, but as God would have it, they happened. I believe the most important part is how I came out of those situations. It was at this time; the Lord began to help me with my understanding by praying and studying scriptures.

"Wherefore be ye not unwise, but understanding what the will of the Lord is" (Ephesians 5:17).

"Consider that I say; and the Lord give thee understanding in all things" (II Timothy 2: 7).

"Let my cry come near before thee, O Lord: give me understanding according to thy word" (Psalms 119:169).

"But there is a spirit in man; and the inspiration of the Almighty giveth them understanding" (Job 32:8).

"Forsake the foolish and live; and go in the way of understanding" (Proverbs 9:6).

"Trust in the Lord with all thine heart; and lean not unto thine own understanding" (Proverbs 3:5).

After reading, studying, and writing about understanding, I had some clarity. I needed an understanding for myself at that time of despair in my life. However, as I reflect upon it now, it wasn't necessarily for me. As I've said before, everything in my life is done on purpose. The Lord gave me understanding on a situation so that I can be a help to others, especially women. I now understand I can't step outside of the will of God and not expect struggle.

In getting my understanding, I began to realize there was so much I wanted from God! I believe that God can do exceedingly above anything that I can ever ask of Him; if I would just ask. I had taken that for granted because I believed that God would give me the desires of my heart without asking. I never petitioned God for those things. The Lord shifted my studies to those scriptures where He encourages us to ask of Him.

"Hitherto have ye asked nothing in my name: ask, and ye shall receive that your joy may be full" (John 16:24).

"If ye shall ask anything in my name, I will do it" (John 14:14).

"And all things whatsoever ye shall ask in prayer, believing, ye shall receive" (Matthew 21:22).

"And whatsoever we ask, we receive of him because we keep his commandments and do those things that are pleasing in his sight" (I John 3:22).

"If ye abide in me, and my words abide in you, ye shall ask what ye will, and it shall be done unto you" (John 15:7).

In reading those scriptures I started to understand how to present things to God. I started to understand the importance of living for God, the power of prayer, and the need to ask God for help. I always thought, "God knows." and He does, but I had to be reminded to ask. Those scriptures remind me that I must ask in His Name and believe that I shall receive. I can honestly say it was easy to ask, but I struggled to believe. The struggle to believe God would provide was the result of not being able to see past what was in front of me. That is where I had to implement my faith and trust God throughout the process.

After getting my understanding and learning how to go to God to ask, I needed to be restored. I needed the Lord to restore my joy, my peace, my heart, and my spirit. The Lord led me to study these scriptures because my growth in Christ depended upon my restoration.

"Restore unto me the joy of thy salvation; and uphold me with thy free spirit" (Psalms 51:12).

"Therefore if any man be in Christ, he is a new creature: old things are passed away; behold, all things are become new" (II Corinthians 5:17).

"And I will restore to you the years that the locust hath eaten, the cankerworm, and the caterpillar, and the palmerworm, my great army which I sent among you" (Joel 2:25).

When I studied on restoration, I was so broken. I was in such a low place that I knew only the Lord could bring me out. I struggled to pick myself back up and believe that God would restore me. It took praying and meditating on God's Word, but He did it. It wasn't overnight, but I'm grateful that He made me anew.

Remember: understanding, asking, and restoring. If you seek God for understanding, trust that He will provide the answers you need. Don't be afraid to ask in Jesus' Name and trust that you will receive. Lastly, God can restore everything that you've lost. It all goes back to having faith and trusting that God will not fail you in your time of need.

When I wrote this almost four years ago, I didn't understand why I had to study the importance of being obedient to the Lord. Please keep in mind, I moved in with a man who wasn't my husband after the Lord told me not to do it. The result of my disobedience led to so many things going wrong in my life. I found other ways to cope while I was still in the relationship, but I could never shake the feeling of knowing that God was not pleased with the life I was living. Initially going into the situation, I thought it would be okay. I was wrong; every day was a struggle. Here are some of the scriptures I studied on obedience.

"And Samuel said, Hath the Lord as great delight in burnt offerings and sacrifices, as in obeying the voice of the Lord? Behold, to obey is better than sacrifice, and to hearken than the fat of rams." (I Samuel 15:22)

"Though he were a Son, yet he learned obedience by the things he suffered" (Hebrews 5:8).

"As obedient children, not fashioning yourselves according to the former lusts in your ignorance" (I Peter 1:14).

"But as he which hath called you is holy, so be ye holy in all manner conversation" (I Peter 1:15).

"Because it is written, Be ye holy; for I am holy" (I Peter 1:16).

I have learned that it is important to be obedient to God's Word. I was raised in a single-parent home, but in all the years after my parents divorced, my mom never had another man in our home. I knew it was not God's Will and I continued to rationalize that it would be alright because I felt that man was my husband.

After realizing the importance of obedience, the Lord led me to study husbands. Now, at the time when He led me to do so, I was confused. I had no idea why I needed to study on husbands because I had in my mind that I was done with relationships and the hopes of marriage were long gone. Be that as it may, I had to be obedient. There are many scriptures on husbands, wives, and marriages, but I will share those that stood out to me.

"Husbands, love your wives and be not bitter against them" (Colossians 3:19).

"For the husband is the head of the wife, even as Christ is the head of the church: and he is the savior of the body." (Ephesians 5:23)

"So ought men to love their wives as their own bodies. He that loveth his wife, loveth himself." (Ephesians 5: 28).

"For this cause shall a man leave his father and mother, and shall be joined unto his wife, and they two shall be one flesh." (Ephesians 5:31).

Initially, I didn't see the point to study, read, and write on husbands. Now four years later, I get it. I've never been married, but I knew back then what I desired in a potential husband. I believe that God must be in any relationship, but especially marriage. I tried to see something in a person that didn't have a desire to go to church, didn't want to pray, and didn't have a relationship with God. When I learned those three things alone, I should have run away as quickly as I could.

I've never had the desire to live with any man who was not my husband. But the devil had me convinced that I was getting older and I would never get married, so I settled. I tried to change a person who had no desire to change. While I was in the situation, I suffered a great deal. I didn't sleep, I stopped communicating with my loved ones, and my kids were miserable. I have learned that a man who loves God will treat me as such. It will show in his character, his actions, and the way he engages me. I decided to be true to myself and what I believe. I know God's Word and it does not return void. After all of that, I had to learn to be content and love myself. I stopped focusing on the fact I was nearing 40 and giving in to the fear of growing old alone. I started enjoying and getting to know Leda.

Once I came to that place, the Lord didn't stop. He continued to lead me to study and write. I started studying patience. Patience is so relevant for me because I'm one who tries to resolve my own issues, instead of waiting on the Lord. I will share some of the scriptures that spoke to me and helped me to be still and hear God.

"Strengthened with all might, according to his glorious power, unto all patience and longsuffering with joyfulness" (Colossians 1: 11).

"Better is the end of a thing than the beginning thereof: and the patient in spirit is better than the proud in spirit" (Ecclesiastes 7:8).

"But in all things approving ourselves as the ministers of God, in much patience, in afflictions, in necessities, in distresses" (II Corinthians 6:4).

It is human nature to be inpatient. We are all guilty of trying to resolve life's issues on our own. I am especially guilty and I took the same approach with relationships. I couldn't wait on the Lord and trust that He would give me my heart's desire in a companion. I consistently tried it on my own and failed. My lesson in patience was not only learning to wait on the Lord from a spiritual perspective, but I had to be patient and not give in to the loneliness I felt. Sometimes waiting on the Lord means longsuffering and trusting God throughout the process.

Lastly, after going through all of what I did, I needed some encouragement. I struggled to stay motivated and encouraged that God would turn everything around. Because of that struggle, I started studying encouragement. Not only did I need it, my children did as well. Here are a few relevant scriptures on encouragement.

"In the day when I cried thou answeredst me, and strengthenedst me with strength in my soul" (Psalm 138:3).

"Have I not commanded thee? Be strong and of a good courage; be not afraid, neither be thou dismayed: for the Lord thy God is with thee whithersoever thou goest" (Joshua 1:9).

"That I may come unto you with joy by the will of God, and may with you be refreshed" (Romans 15:32).

"But they that wait upon the Lord shall renew their strength; they shall mount up with wings as eagles; they shall run, and not be weary; and they shall walk and not faint" (Isaiah 40:31).

I am so encouraged by God's word and his promises. I have come a long way over the past four years and God has shown up in my life in ways I never imagined. After getting to a place where I felt like I was totally broken, God still didn't forget about me. Instead He reminded me to be strong, trust Him to heal my soul and my heart, hold on to my faith, get an understanding, and ask Him for my heart desires so He could restore me and make me whole again. Just when I thought He was done, the Lord reminded me about the importance of being obedient, trusting Him for my husband, being patient enough to let Him work on my behalf, and learning to be encouraged through it all.

Chapter Eleven: Moving Beyond the Pain

After all of that, God was not done with me! He placed transition in my spirit. It was time for a fresh start. I prayed about it and asked the Lord to lead me to a place where I could live in my purpose. I started looking for jobs in Tennessee. I initially thought I was going to Memphis, but then I thought Nashville was the place for me. So, I started sending my resumes to potential employers there. Little did I know God had a different plan. I was at a place where I was no longer a victim and I was excited about my future.

I continued to apply for jobs and the response was very slow. But, I didn't give up hope. It seemed like things at my current job were getting stressful and I almost wanted to give up on finding a job. I remember one day my mom told me, "Leda, blossom where you are. Until God moves you, just blossom where you are." That's just what I did. I made it my business to go above and beyond on my job. I stopped complaining about how I was ready to go and focused on being positive and trusting that all things were in God's timing. When I did that, God opened the door. I was at work one day and I received a call about a job I'd applied for months prior. It was the supervisor and she basically did an initial phone interview before scheduling a face-to face-interview via Skype. I could not believe it! I was so excited to see what God was going to do.

The day of the Skype interview arrived and I was a nervous wreck. I went to my friend's house to use her laptop because mine was on its last leg. After what seems like forever, the interview was over and I had to wait. The interview was for a position with one of the top universities in the world, so my potential supervisor warned me how the human resources department could sometimes not move as quickly as she'd like. Nevertheless, I knew whatever the outcome, it was God's will. In the meantime, I was continuing to blossom on my job. There were days I wanted to give up because it seemed as if every obstacle was coming my way. But, I didn't give up. I was praying and letting the Lord fight my battles. I'd learned my lesson about trying to resolve my problems on my own.

By now it was late summer of 2014, and my supervisor, a few other colleagues, and I were preparing to travel to Washington D.C. for a conference. The week I was scheduled to leave, I received a call from my potential supervisor, who offered me a face-to-face interview. I was ecstatic to say the least! I scheduled the interview the day after I returned from Washington because I was off work. My mom thought I was crazy because the interview was about four-and-a-half hours away and she insisted I would be too tired to drive. She was 100 percent correct, but I was determined. I went to Washington with my colleagues, enjoyed the conference, saw some of my former colleagues, and one of my best friends. I met some new people, and even saw one of my classmates from college. It was my first time flying and my first time in Washington, D.C. While I enjoyed the trip, I was eager for it to be over.

After I returned from D.C., I could hardly contain myself. My mom picked me up at the airport and I stayed over at her place so she could keep my kids while I went to the interview. I will admit that after that long flight, I was exhausted, but I wouldn't dare tell my mom that. The day of the interview arrived and I was well-rested and ready to tackle the road. The drive was long, but I arrived 45 minutes ahead of schedule. I was fine with that because I had a chance to pull over, get out of the car, stretch, and put on my make-up. I went to the office where my interview was to take place, and my nerves were getting the best of me. I said a prayer, asked the Lord to go before me, and let His Will be done. I interviewed with my potential supervisor and three potential colleagues. It seemed like the interview took forever, but I walked out of it with confidence. I'd done my part and the rest was up to God. I had nothing, but positive thoughts on my ride back home.

As I resumed my normal routine, I'd hoped for some good news soon. During the interview the program supervisor stated that the university had to go through its process; complete reference checks, verify my current employment, and determine a salary. She was unsure when she would be in contact with me. I could only hope for the best. I was not worried because God's time is not like man's time. It was a few weeks, but I got a call one day from my potential supervisor with an offer for employment and salary quote. She expressed that she'd never known the university to complete the process for a new hire so quickly. I knew it was God's favor. After accepting the offer, everything else moved along. I accepted the position in Knoxville, TN, so the following weekend my dad, niece, and I went to look for apartments. That Monday, I turned in my two-week notice to my supervisor, scheduled my exit interview, and gave notice to my landlord. It was all happening so fast. I could not believe it.

It was the day before the move, and I was nervous. I let my kids go to school because I had to go pick up my moving truck and get everything loaded. My dad was supposed to pick me up and ride with me to get the truck, but as usual, he was late. I had a reservation, so I went to pick the truck up and I had no driver. Ugh! I was so frustrated with my dad for being late. Nevertheless, I picked up my niece because she was a truck driver at the time, so I figured she wouldn't mind driving the truck back to my apartment. We made it back to my apartment and started to load the truck. I knew it wouldn't be easy because I'm very OCD about my things; my dad and my brother tend to be careless. My nerves were on edge while we loaded the truck and my nerves were shot by the time we were finished. It took what seemed like hours, but we got everything done in preparation for the move the next day.

It was finally moving day and I was still a nervous wreck. I didn't have the exact money I needed to move in and I was determined not to ask my dad. I didn't know how, but I would come up with something. My dad arrived at my apartment and we packed the last items on the truck before leaving. After doing a final check in the apartment and turning in my keys, we went on our way. Our first stop was my mom's house because she was going with me to stay a few weeks until I was settled. When we arrived at my mom's house, she could see I was in a panic. I told her I still didn't get the rest of the money I needed, but I was going ahead anyway. My mom looked at me, and politely walked over to my dad. She pulled him aside and explained to him the situation and asked him to give me the rest of the money I needed. He agreed to do so and just like that my problem was solved.

After saying a word a prayer for traveling grace, we started on our six-hour trip to Knoxville. I had completed my paperwork for my apartment via email and fax, so I was anxious to see it in reality for the first time. My kids were anxious and kind of sad too. I realized it was a difficult move for them, but they would appreciate it later, I hoped. I was excited about the idea of a fresh start and having a sense of normalcy for my family. I knew in my heart this was not only my last move, but it would be my best move.

We arrived at my apartment complex and I was beyond excited. My parents, kids, and I walked into the office to meet with an agent to sign my lease. It was all so surreal; I had to contain my emotions! I'd come a long way from where I started.

After completing the paperwork, we found my building and my apartment. As I put the key in the door to unlock it, I was overcome with emotions. I walked in with my mom and as we looked around, I began to cry. I loved my new place! It was more than I had imagined and just the right size for my little family. But more than that, I was crying because God didn't give up on me. I stood there crying; I could hear my mom walking around and praising God. She was saying, "This is it. God has something great in store for you, Leda. Just don't give up and keep holding on." As I stood there still in tears, I was looking forward to starting my new life in Knoxville. I was told as a single mother, I couldn't make it, I was statistically meant to live on welfare and not have anything. I was determined to beat those odds because I believed I could. What God did for me is nothing short of amazing. He saved me, healed my heart, and restored me. I can only hope that sharing my story of pain encourages you to look beyond your circumstances, trust God for your healing and find your purpose through it all.

Acknowledgements

I truly give God all the praise because He gave me the gift of writing. My children, Emily, Emmanuel and Lydia, you all are my life, my source of strength and my motivation. It is because of you, that I never gave up. I love you all with every ounce of my being! I thank my parents, Paul and Ruby Porter, who never agreed on much, but forced me to go back to college and get my degree. You saw something in me, even when I didn't. I'm forever grateful God gave me you. My siblings, Ramona, Yanda, Paula, Demarco and Tiffany, thank you for your support over the years. Love you all! My best friend Kashayla, you are amazing! It's been 17 years and you've remained the same. I so appreciate you and your constant encouragement and support. My mentor Twannia, what can I say? I owe you my life! You never gave up on me and you saw the potential and the call the Lord had on my life even before I accepted it. Thank you for praying for me, never judging me and lifting me up when I was down. Love you! My friends Kaile and Jayson, I must acknowledge you because you ministered to me about writing my story when I had given up on doing so. I will never forget how the Lord used you to minister to me that night years ago. Your words of encouragement blessed me more than you will ever know. To all my family and friends near or far who have supported me over the years, thank you from the bottom of my heart! I can't list each of you individually, but you know who you are and the bond we share. I thank God for the prayers, vast support, and words of encouragement. May God, bless you all!

Made in the USA
Columbia, SC
19 October 2017